Jolita

Steinberg Henry

Gotham Books

30 N Gould St.
Ste. 20820, Sheridan, WY 82801
https://gothambooksinc.com/

Phone: 1 (307) 464-7800

© 2025 *Steinberg Henry*. All rights reserved.

No part of this book may be reproduced, stored in a retrieval system, or transmitted by any means without the written permission of the author.

Published by Gotham Books (February 19, 2025)

ISBN: 979-8-3485-1744-1 (H)
ISBN: 979-8-3484-9408-7 (P)
ISBN: 979-8-3484-9409-4 (E)

Because of the dynamic nature of the Internet, any web addresses or links contained in this book may have changed since publication and may no longer be valid.

The views expressed in this work are solely those of the author and do not necessarily reflect the views of the publisher, and the publisher hereby disclaims any responsibility for them.

Prologue

She is twenty-six; he's sixty. They never met except by way of their voices and emails. Over a three-year period, the two communicate, one in Georgia, USA, and the other in the Eastern Caribbean island of Dominica.

She is a mother of one; he's a father of four. She's single; he's married. In the context of cultural and religious beliefs, these exchanges are unacceptable. She has a boyfriend; he has a wife.

But she's caring beyond her age. It is the mature soul in her that captures his emotions and fires his psyche.

In this exchange of letters, you'll feel the pace as trust grows and the relationship deepens. In truth, the text is profound, intimate, philosophical, full of love, and mutual care.

In the context of island-state culture, the question "who is Jolita" is sure to arise. Do not judge her. Read her intelligence and fearlessness as she dares to love and show her concern for a man whose youngest child is older than her.

She is a true mother-spirit, a wholesome feminine, a daring woman who broke into a state of seeing and knowing that did not concern itself about the rules and simply looked into herself to discover elements of her life's purpose and subsequently move on.

The dates of the letters, the writer, and a special island fruit introduce each correspondence. The exchanges take off in March 2015.

And let there be no purpose in friendship save the deepening of the spirit.

—Kahlil Gibran, *The Prophet*

March 25, 2015

Jolita

I can't really imagine how difficult it must be for you, someone who has always seen the world through his eyes, having to find another eye to see the world through. It must have really been a challenge for you. I do believe that things happen for a reason. You see things that other people will fail to see.

You read people from the inside and not just from what they look like. You have accomplished things you would have never thought of embarking into if you had your sight. You have helped people and showed people another way to look at life, from the inside out. You have been an inspiration to so many people, and I believe it doesn't stop there. See it not as a curse but as a blessing.

July 14, 2015

Stein

When is your birthday?

July 14, 2015

Jolita

Good morning,

How are you doing? I miss hearing your voice. How are things with you? How is the family?

I will be getting my phone by next week, so we can talk.

My birthday is _____. Have a blessed day today.

Remember, in all things seek God first. Nothing happens by accident. He always has a plan. It's up to you to find out what that plan is.

July 20, 2015

Stein

Remember to collect a copy of my book *Calypso Drift* at Choices Bookstore. It's your birthday gift.

I spoke with the store about it already. You simply need to show some form of ID.

Again, love to you, and remember, you came into this world equipped with all that you need inside you. Write soon.

—St.

July 20, 2015

Jolita

Good morning, Mr. Henry,

Thank you so much for the gift. I really do appreciate it. Wishing you a blessed day today and God's guidance and grace.

August 10, 2015

Jolita

I have started reading your book. I find it very interesting so far. I haven't gotten far as yet, but your adventures throughout your life are too much. You are too brave! You have lived a life, one full of adventure and discoveries. The people you met along your way just made the journey worth taking. They have added to the journey, whether it be in a positive way or just a minor setback. Either way, it pointed you in the direction you needed to go and grow with a more steady and focused mind. I don't see how I would have ever gone on that ship. I am not that motivated. I view my life as too precious to risk.

The way we sometimes look at situations in life blinds us to the bigger picture. It blinds us from seeing the emotion behind a story. In literature, we say you need to learn to read between the lines, but in life we need to see beyond the picture, beyond what the normal eyes see. Sometimes all we need to do is close our eyes and feel a situation, smell it, breathe it in, taste it, live it, then and only then can we see, really understand the situation.

Life has not always been easy. Who would have thought that your journey in life would have landed you here? You have accomplished so much in life so far, and yet with your limitation, you are still touching lives; you are inspiring people on so many levels.

That one man who has been all over, studying, one day hoping to be the best at what he does, suddenly finds a different life story. No one would have seen this coming. One minor difficulty has opened doors to so many other opportunities. Where others would have given up, you stood up. Keep aspiring. Keep writing and encouraging. You are an inspiration, a great person, and a great friend. Enjoy your day today.

August 10, 2015

Jolita

Good morning,

I must say that you know how to have me choking on laughter. It's not that easy to contain. How are you this morning? Did you get some rest?

How is the natural healing process working for you so far? I know it takes a lot of patience, but how is it working for you thus far?

August 10, 2015

Stein

You're absolutely right—it is a natural healing process. Processes take time; this is where the problem is encountered both in terms of the physical/physiological phenomenon and the person's state of mind or psychological process. In fact, in the case of this latter, I may well choose to say, the person's psyche.

I have been able to keep a reasonable plant based meal, complemented with nuts, seeds, fruits, and any edible bit of natural food that has remained generally uncontaminated in the United States. I am not even sure about bottled water. In the process, not only have I been forced to fast as often as I can or even to move my thoughts into positive places; I must say that I have had to draw on spiritual nutrition. Spiritual nutrition. Hmmm. I would really like you to tell me what you think this means. Just write… can't wait.

My massage therapy friend visited a few weeks ago, and he looked at me and said, "Stein, you look healthy." I looked at him thinking that he might be flattering because my eyes are still misty white or dark. He continued, "I can tell when a person is healthy." So in truth, it is really a process, and that takes time and energy.

I've found that my sleep is deep at times and interrupted at other times, mainly by sudden movements out of sleep to find an idea. Thing is, the creative process will not stop even if I see or not, and this, in effect, gives me reason for believing that someday I shall come upon an epiphany, an aha moment.

That will be the day when the energy of the Holy Spirit—yes, the Holy Spirit is energy in our bodies—

and its tremendous body of energy, an infinite source, will reveal to me the formula. There is cure/healing, but that will not be in pharmaceuticals or in the present medical profession, though a few brave souls are emerging to speak about age-old remedies buried because of profiteers and their greed.

Over and beyond this politics, I feel fine, just completing editing of a book on behalf of Jahlee, the beautiful singer from Grandbay. She has collected over eighty short stories about NYC and her own homeland, DA. As for me, I take this writing to you and your responses seriously.

In addition, a number of topics are rising for attention. When it's all said and reflected on, I should have a masterpiece in the making as my fifth book. I boast, I must say, in Christ! Oh, Stein, negate this comfortable zone and reach into your own self—the abundant gift in and of the human spirit. I write this and know that I am connected to and in that vastness called the universe, and it alone does not move me. There's a Spirit, and I love it!

I am also looking forward to the repair of my bike, on which I do a major cardio—between thirty and forty-five minutes riding. Hey, that's indoors! A small part was chipped, and that made riding noisy. The part is here; my partner just has to replace the old, broken one. That, he said, should be soon. As soon as this happens, I should be into another physical mode—a strengthening.

Write me soon and write as much as you can.

August 11, 2015

Jolita

Hi,

It's great that you are still hanging in there and focusing on your healing. Focus on your healing. Let not the lengthy process discourage you.

It's about the fight, the fight for freedom from this disability, but while living with it, open your ears to the music, to the sounds around you, to the "rid dim" of its beat. Like in your book, on that boat, the music had its own story to tell. So does this challenge. So listen.

You seem to be more healthy than you expect. You eat well, you exercise, and the fact that your mind is always at work is a plus for you. Keep it up. You do more than most people. I try to keep healthy, but I hate eating and have little to no time to exercise. So keep it up.

The healing secrets from our ancestors had to be lost in time. If they were kept alive, there would be little to no sicknesses. Our ancestors experimented a lot. A lot of lives were lost to experiments; things like these should be carried down through generations, but they were not. They got lost along the way.

Spiritual nutrition—that's a topic I think can be viewed from different angles. To me, I see it as anything that would nourish the spirit. We are considered spiritual beings taking residence in this fleshly body. I believe that as we are to nourish the fleshly body with food and water, so too should we nourish the spiritual body with spiritual things. I believe meditation of the mind is a good way. Putting the fleshly body to rest well, you then focus only on your spiritual body—feeding your mind with things to uplift your spirit, filling your mind with the great amazing wonders of life, and concentrating only on that. I believe it's trying to make that spiritual connection: your spirit to the other peaceful spirits around you.

The spirits in the universe call out, but we are too busy to hear. You need to relax and listen; let the communication between good spirits nourish your spirit and in return, heal your fleshly body. It's not by might, not by power, but by the Spirit, says the Lord.

Have yourself a blessed day.

August 11, 2015

Stein

I must address you in your full capacity as cowriter and cocommunicant in this process of self-unfolding. It is a pleasure to find a Dominican woman willing and making time to write about matters touching history, healing, disability, the body, the spirit, and who knows where next this ship will travel to, its next port of entry, given that its sailing narrative is effortless...

You write deep. You cause me to want to leave the text and return to it later, but to speak the truth, I am moved by your insight. Didn't start this way. It —seems to me that you too, needed to write. I can feel your narrative as it slowly reveals its constitution— the body, healing, sound, patient process, and most of all, the spirit of the living God. Respect, sister!

You wrote, "(F)ocus on your healing, let not the lengthy process discourage you. It is about the fight, the fight for freedom from this disability, but while living with it, open your ears to the music, to the sounds around you, to the 'riddim' of its beat. Like in your book, on that boat the music had its own story to tell. So does this challenge. So listen." Were you speaking about the Jamaica scene on that Nicaraguan boat at Port Royal? It is amazing that you should catch this. It is a very special "heart" moment, but also, it is a technical moment when the producer has to be listening to the subtle, observing the background and not just what figures, keeping in mind all along the purpose of the entire project—to produce a program that informs. This is a beautiful lesson in listening so nicely hidden in Calypso Drift and, of course, extrapolated by you and your power of observation.

As for the process which we seem to come upon in our exchange, I have been to the point where I feel my body unable to contain my spirit. I just blow out and wash my face. At those moments, my sight is all white, all around me is white. I cannot see my fingers in front my eyes, My point of reference remains me and the body I think I have. Yes, the body I think I have.

Beyond its presence, its existence which I am aware of, beyond this surface, everything outside of me is null and white. There are days when it is dark. Well, a human being has to have courage to survive darkness. Not only is it thick under the brightest sun; it feels like it wants to choke. In times like these, I enter deeper darkness. I move my meditation beyond the body's darkness into the Spirit's light because beyond the darkness of the flesh is the light of the Spirit. Here, there is beauty!

And then again, when you say what follows below, I think that I need look carefully at myself and sense of self to determine whether I am not doing better than I think. You write, "(Y)ou seem to be healthier than you expect. You eat well, you exercise, and the fact that your mind is always at work is a plus for you. Keep it up. You do more than most people. I try to keep healthy, but I hate eating and have little to no time to exercise."

You're going to have to give me a description of yourself. What is your height, weight, color of skin, hair length, color of eyes? Wow. This is asking much. I must be discreet in this matter since I do not want to be invasive. I need remember that this woman is a future criminal lawyer. But imagine, I cannot see you clearly and need an impression of you.

Do you like nuts—all kinds of nuts? I mean walnuts, almonds, cashew, peanuts, etc. This is good for eating. Then you should sip liquids, prepare vegetable soups. Tell me what you like eating, and I will find recipes for you. You must eat something. A woman has to have some flesh on her body, my mother used to say. I do not think she meant getting fat or gorging over and above what one's stomach can contain or eating all that junk, but of course, I think in addition to eating that which pleases you, your spirit and disposition have to be seminal in your growth and development.

You're absolutely right when you say "(T)he healing secrets from our ancestors had to be lost in time; if they were kept alive, there would be little to no sicknesses. Our ancestors experimented a lot. A lot of lives were lost to experiments; things like these should be carried down through generations, but they were not.." All I can say is, how insightful! You should know all the herbs in and around your yard. Those for teas and those for cooking. You know in Dominica, we used to sweeten our teas in the morning. I gather it's still being done. After hanging out with Chinese for a few years at university, I observed that they do not, absolutely do not sweeten their teas. Takes a bit to taste, but after a while, I came to appreciate the tea's aroma and the herb's enriching oil. Drink bush tea, and if you can't take it without sweetening, use a drop of honey for flavoring.

Then there was the question which emerged in our last mail. You wrote most magnificently,

> "Spiritual nutrition—that's a topic I think can be viewed from different angles. To me, I see it as anything that would nourish the spirit. We are considered spiritual beings taking residence in this fleshly body. I believe that as we are to nourish the fleshly body with food and water, so too we

should nourish the spiritual body with spiritual things."

I can only say at this juncture, since I am sure the matter will continue to arise in our communications, that the spirit has harvested an abundance of nutrition just for our safety and well-being. We, as moderns, were not trained to look to that abundance, and now we have the "sweet trouble" to align ourselves, to source, to tap into that metasource. It is written that the Holy Spirit—the most awesome source of energy—is a deposit. Yes, a deposit in lieu of that larger amount. It is available starting now.

Then you suggest how it could be tapped. You note, "(I) believe meditation of the mind is a good way. Putting the fleshly meditated body to rest well, requires that you focus only on your spiritual body, feeding your mind with things to uplift your spirit, filling your mind with the great amazing wonders of life and concentrating only on that. I believe it's trying to make that spiritual connection: your spirit to the other peaceful spirits around you."

You should read Hebrews 12 when Paul writes about the "cloud of witnesses." They can be seen forming among stars. When we were at school, we plotted charts on a x and y line. Stars take up shape, and then out of the shape they take appears a human form, replacing the plotted stars. That witness does not stand on anything and walks on air. Our people are all around us.

As you said, and rightly so, "(T)he spirits in the universe call out, but we are too busy to hear. You need to relax and listen; let the communication between good spirits nourish your spirit and in return, heal your fleshly body. It's not by might, not by power, but by the spirit, says the Lord." Amen, sister!

Good spirits, good thought. Also, thinking what you want for yourself is key. Bob Marley once sang, "Go to hell if what you're thinking is not right." Having written this, the question becomes, now that we know these things, why are we not totally healthy, healed, or cured? Takes us back to the matter of process which you write on so eloquently. You're amazing, you know. Do you meditate?

August 12, 2015

Stein

I needed to return to a few specifics in what you wrote. This statement below is loaded, given modern culture's irreversible focus on social media, telecommunications, and gadgets. In the process, narcissism rises, stress surges, the grid tightens, and relationships slither into nothingness lacking intimacy.

Listening is a rare practice, may well have become commodity—persons are looking for someone to tell them how to listen. Human beings all over the world have not been trained to look into themselves. The practice has certainly come late to the Western world. I heard the government of India is seeking to protect its ancient yoga techniques from being trademarked by Western countries. There is an eagerness to look inside. Thank God, there are those of us who came to know it.

Listening. I've learned that we do not listen only with our ears. We listen and hear with our bones too. It is something you should observe. Think it was well-captured by one musician who spoke of the music being felt in the bones. V. S. Naipaul was said to be a powerful writer because he listened so intensely. You wrote, "(T)he spirits in the universe call out, but we are too busy to hear…" " Distractions are massive. Spirits in the universe need stillness. And when you think of it, the universe itself has its sound. Just imagine the sound of the universe entering your ears, skin, and bones. We are wrapped in loving sounds unto eternity, but our human-created sounds challenge our wallets, redefine time and sell us pharmaceuticals.

Sound of the universe? When you read Psalm 8, there is the verse which says, "When I consider the heavens, the work of your fingers, the moon and stars." I understood a hurricane has been raging on Jupiter for the last three hundred years! Jupiter's diameter is said to be eleven times larger than Earth and according to NASA Science the planet has 95 moons! It is said too that the River Nile meanders in a shape similar to the universe Milky Way! The Nile circles Ethiopia three times!

"You need to relax and listen. Let the communication between good spirits nourish your spirit and in return heal." Excellent counsel. I continue the practice. It is the only way to health and healing.

August 13, 2015

Jolita

Good morning,

I took so long to reply. I just couldn't concentrate. You are such an inspiration to me. I don't really express myself this way to anybody. Talking on issues is not something I like to do, but I feel free to express myself with you.

Sometimes I sit, I think of what it is like to sit in complete darkness, afraid of what lies beyond this darkness. The peace there may be, but the fear of the unknown surrounding can be real scary, I would suppose.

This extract from your email really got me to a level where I feel like I need to reach this point in life. "I move my meditation beyond the body's darkness into the Spirit's light because, beyond the darkness of the flesh is the light of the Spirit. Here, there is beauty."

I want to feel that beauty that exists there. I know there is beauty, but with our busy lives, we consume ourselves with things of the flesh and never make time for the things of the Spirit.

I do not meditate at all. I can't really find the time to just cast everything aside for that one sweet moment. I would love to, but I always find myself consumed with distractions. I do not like eating, but it's not because of my size. I just don't find foods here intriguing to my taste buds. It's like the same things over and over again, prepared differently but still the same. Right now I am trying something more Spanish, in terms of the seasonings and spices. I have a love for the Spanish cultures, music, and dance, so I'm trying the food. Hopefully that will give me the difference I am looking for.

As for the sugar in tea, I have cut down on it a little but still taking sugars. Can't really avoid it. I eat nuts, but when it comes to veggies, I can't take them in. It's a mental thing, I know, but it's taking me a little time to get over it. I am working on it. I am just not a food person.

I am not so small in body. I am actually quite thick. Not fat but thick. I am about 5'2" in height, dark-skinned, dark brown eyes, and straightened hair just below shoulder length.

I am the ideal short, thick Dominican black girl. Have yourself a blessed day today. Hoping to hear from you soon

August 13, 2015

Jolita

Good morning,

The way you look at life is so enriching. Your thoughts on listening…

Listening is a process that we seem too busy to complete. We hear things with our ears, and we therefore shape our actions, thoughts, and life based mainly on what we hear—we do not listen to the sounds and the music around us.

Modern culture has had a drastic impact on our development as a person and as a nation. The things that are put in place every day for our entertainment and even for our development have somehow distracted our lives in a way that forces us to see, hear and feel things from the surface, unable to go further as to reading between the lines and seeing beyond the basic eye. Glasses and hearing aids, no matter how strong, cannot help with this issue. It can only help you focus less on your business and more on your neighbors. These are the things that destroy our society today. As you clearly stated out, "This statement below is loaded, given modern culture's irreversible focus on social media, telecommunications, and gadgets. In the process, narcissism rises, stress surges, the grid tightens and relationships slither into nothingness lacking intimacy."

Yes, the government of India is being smart in trying to protect its ancient yoga techniques, 'cause in it there is healing, self-realization, and peace. I just hope like ancient medicines, it is not lost through the generations. They have realized that their techniques are being copied and modified, losing the essence of its own being. Yoga is a spiritual thing, like a religion, though other states have changed the meaning of yoga. It's not just a meditation. It is a worship. It is spirit communicating with spirits.

I've heard about listening with the heart but never yet have I heard about listening with your bones. This one is new to me. Very captivating thought. I am going to try this one. I try listening with every part of me—I hate missing a thing at times. There is so much out there that we just can't hear. The best of things we miss.

Listening is just one of the things in this life that's so hard to perfect, and sadly we don't even try. The book of Psalms talks so much about the beauty of the things we are yet to see. Not only in a psalm but throughout the Bible, the universe is described and all its beauties. It paints an amazing picture that we should all try to get a glance of every now and then. Can't wait to hear from you.

August 14, 2015

Stein

Good day again.

It's Friday, and I'm smiling, dropping this non-philosophical note. It is one of those mornings when I must go back to sleep. It's not that I woke up particularly early, but I became a bit depressed last night after my grandson came home with his father, and traces of eczema, which he had and which were clearing, seemed to have returned. And he was scratching. This intensification began when he was returned to day care.

I hate to see and hear children cry over discomforts of the body. I just don't know what to do. Or maybe I should say, I do what I have to do to cure him with my breath, mind, and spirit, but I must say, I tend to want immediate ease for him. He's seven months.

How much more terrible are mothers feeling, helpless, holding a few pounds in their hands as he screams sometimes. I gather you know this much better than me.

I think he's going to be okay. After all, he's a well fed baby, but just the moment, just that moment of discomfort unnerved me, annoyed me, and had me wondering about pediatricians and dermatologists—how they're trained and what they learn and why they cannot cure. Much love to you over this weekend and care your little one... You wouldn't believe just two days ago, I had gone back to my favorite Psalm, Psalm 8, to read the section/verse about children—out of the mouths of babes and sucklings, etc. The versions vary.

I spent quite a bit of time in meditation, trying to fathom how is it that God uses children to stop an enemy, or how is it that God uses the praises of children to stop savagery of an enemy. It then occurred to me that innocence is powerful. Those who are without sin can move mountains. My father used to tell me in time, children will walk on atom bombs. I gather he meant nuclear ones. It is the power of innocence. Observe that innocence brings with it effortlessness, stillness, intuition. Watch him when he plays. I wish you a wonderful weekend and as always, look forward to reading you, and just in case I miss this—I love the "ideal" girl. I love her even more when she describes herself as "thick" and "dark!"

August 14, 2015

Jolita

Good day,

It's so nice hearing from you.

I'm so sorry about your grandson. That's so horrible. I don't know why kids have to go through so much pain at such a tender age. It is heartbreaking. The mother must be feeling miserable in a time like this. I would be.

I remember when my son used to get gripes at a tender age. I couldn't sleep. I didn't know what to do., I couldn't help him at all. All I could do was cry and pray that this would soon end. Thank God for my mother. She really helped me through it. She used to put my son to sleep every night and be up with him no matter the time. I used to tell her, Now I know why he didn't want to come out of me. He knew the suffering and pain that was in store." All you can do now is be there for him and help him not to scratch. He is going to be okay. Something at the day care maybe triggered his eczema, but it will soon clear out. We just have to pray and hope it doesn't get triggered again. Have yourself a blessed day and a great weekend.

August 17, 2015

Jolita

Hey,

Good morning. How are you today? How is your grandson doing? I Hope he is a lot better today. Thought of him over the weekend. Prayed for him.

How is your meditation coming along? I tried meditating on Saturday and Sunday, but I haven't gotten the hang of it yet. My thoughts are all over the place.

I am trying to get it under control, but there is so much. I think I have too many "thinks" on my mind. The mind keeps thinking of all sorts of things, never stable. My concentration is very weak. I shall not stop trying 'cause there is a lot of good and positive things that can come from it. Hope you had a blessed day today.

August 17, 2015

Stein

It has been productive so far, though I spent some part of this morning resting. When I wake at four or so, because I write better in that time-space, usually I feel like sleeping after nine or so. And sometimes, I can sleep long. But I'm cool enjoying a much cooler temperature than that of July or the first week of August. Summer... It's a pleasure reading you and thanks for praying. Wow. So young and already, a beautiful young woman is praying for him! Hmmm.

I hope your son is doing well, and of course, since you have become part of my prayer circle, you are lifted up too—you and yours in my meditation and prayer.

Meditation is easy, and when we have the opportunity to speak again—that is, when you're at home—I will tell you a simple technique for dealing with those thoughts. They are yours, so you must embrace them, even while you try focusing... it's what you return to focus on.

I would like to explain by voice/telephone and not by text... as now. Who knows, we may even be able to do a meditation together over distance. Much love to you.

August 18, 2015

Stein

Contrary to what you might have expressed in your very first email to me, when you recommended that I look at sight limitation as a blessing, not as a curse, a woman told me yesterday that blindness is as a result of sin. I was amazed. She is leading member of Seventh-day Adventist. You just can't tell people how to think, even adults.

Hope you're having a day full of interesting discoveries, and please, be gentle with yourself.

August 18, 2015

Jolita

Good day, everyone is entitled to their opinion, but my God, you don't say these stupid things. Does she think for herself? It's unbelievable that someone would say such a thing. It's hard to believe. What about her sins and the sins of others? What is the result of those sins?

As a leader, nonetheless, she is just misleading people then. Blindness can never be the result of sin, else we would all be blind.

Please bear no mind to these people who speak such foolishness. You are better than them. Instead of telling you that, why didn't she just pray with you for God to forgive you of whichever sin she thinks resulted in blindness. Oh, I forgot. They don't pray with people. Ha-ha! Have a blessed day.

August 20, 2015

Stein

It is amazing. I gather they do better praying to their God in the sky, not realizing we're all in the sky! Hey, your perception is prescient.

Just left my guitar, which I keep learning to play, to come to my computer intuiting that there was my buddy saying something wholesome to me. Hope you're well.

It has been a week of change. At present, I am editing a 228-page autobiography for one sister.

Then of course, Jahlee's wonderful collection of New York stories is about to be printed and placed within covers. I read through and edited the entire 299 pages. She is to come up with a cover design by Monday next—she tells me she's stressed trying to think it up. Told her I like when she's in that situation.

She says I'm wicked! Ha-ha! I reminded her that the only reason she feels stressed is because her brain is "downloading" a precise thought chemistry all intended to help resolve the matter. Because it's fresh thought chemistry, it is unusual and so does feel weighty, but as the day ends and the sun disappears from her horizon, the weight will be released. Not all difficulties are solved and resolved this way. I speak of creative challenges.

Don't know why I'm writing this to you. I gather you'll have to come up with a creative solution to a particular problem. Well, that's power-knowledge; that's creative intelligence. Can't wait to teach you meditation.

August 20, 2015

Jolita

Hi, Stein,

How are you today? Hope you are having a good day, reading and cross-checking documents and also writing your own material. I hope that you are making time for yourself also. Work may be important, but your health is even more important. I don't think I would be able to do editing. It is too much reading. I am still not halfway your book as yet. Still trying to get there. I love reading, but the time is never there.

She knows her book. I believe if she can imagine what she writes, she can form a picture in her mind that reflects her book or herself. As long as it's something that she feels, she can feel her book through.

You are wicked in a way. You read the book, you know what it says, and can guide her even better, but you leave her to stress. You know how hard it can be to picture up the right cover. The cover is very important in captivating its readers. It's the first thing you see.

You said, "Don't know why I'm writing this to you. I gather you'll have to come up with a creative solution to a particular problem." I really do hope that I don't have such problems to solve. I'm not good at solving any problems unless if it's mathematical.

It's always a pleasure hearing from you. Have yourself a blessed day.

—J.

August 25, 2015

Jolita

Good morning,

How are you doing this morning? How's the little prince?

How is the weather up there? I hope everything is okay.

Blindness—the Gift of a Spirited Man

He saw with the eyes of the spirit, eyes of the heart, and eyes of the ears. His vision was much more than 20/20, for he saw the unseen, felt the presence everywhere. His sight is blessed, was touched by an angel. He may not see like we see—his sight is much greater. They call him blind; they call it sin, but little do they know it's a gift, it's hidden within. Through those dark closed eyes, there is a vision that sees the unseen. You ask me how. I am yet to comprehend. There is beauty in the unseen: it opens up your eyes from deep within. It's a meditation of the body that only few can achieve.

August 25, 2015

Stein

Wow! This is truly inspired of God! You are truly a beautiful soul inside and within a thick body. How magnificent that you so flawlessly intuited this!

A songwriter once breathed, "I think I love you." I extend these feelings to you and the God of your redemption, who has directed you to meet me along life's banks with these words of eternal power. One day you shall see and know the power in what you've written and be blessed for it.

September 1, 2015

Jolita

Good day,

How are you doing? Just thought I would pop in to say hi. Sometimes in life, we don't really appreciate the value of a friend and friendship. We see friendship as a simple hi and hello. It's more than just that to me; it's the impact that someone leaves on your life. It's the mark that tattoos your heart. That is the impact of a true friendship.

It is said that a good friend is hard to find. I'm glad that I have found a friend in you. Easy to talk to, always putting a smile on my face. You are just a joyous soul. This is something that is not easily found. I thank God for a friend like you.

Continue to be the sweet person that you are, and let your heart continue to warm the people around you.

Have a blessed day today.

With love,

J.

On August 27, 2015, tropical storm Erika hit Dominica. There was destruction of a village, massive flooding, and loss of life

September 2, 2015

Stein

Good day to you too. First, I must hasten to tell you that you need care yourself in this post-Erika environment and its plethora of bacteria in pieces of objects and in the air. I am assured that you will.

I am particularly disturbed by what happened in Dominica, and hopefully one day when we speak or meet for lunch or something, I will tell you a story of interest and intrigue.

Thanks for singling me out as friend. Most of those I call friends are persons I've known long—I never leave wonderful friends. I sensed quite quickly that when we met by telephone on that day—"designed," I assume—I sensed that we were and

going to be knowing each other. We could not leave the line though we had met in conversation for the first time.

You wrote this splendid sentence: "It's the impact that someone leaves on your life. It's the mark that tattoos your heart. That is the impact of a true friendship."

I found the verb *tattoos* in the present tense to be pretty titillating, full of heart's truth and mind's imaginary. There is an indelible quality about its imprint and internalizing. I love the ideas you express.

Remember, we started with criminal law and the law degree. Hope we can revisit this matter someday soon when Dominica has settled down. Be well, magnificent woman. Love!

September 2, 2015

Jolita

Hi

It was really nice hearing your voice today. I am trying my best to take care of myself and my son in this environment. It's horrible, but thank God for life.

I will survive this post-Erika environment. Got me a little sore in the throat, but that is for a moment, it is expected. Dominica got a really bad unexpected hit. Lives and homes were lost, but I thank God for the living. I thank him for life. He gives and he takes in his own time.

The situation is very heartbreaking. Families went to bed and were awakened by flooding and landslides. Children lost parents and vice versa. Families lost their homes and everything in it. The conditions they have to live in today are just heartbreaking, having to start over with nothing. We may not understand why it happened like this or why Dominica, when Erika seemed so far away from us, but he knows. I believe there is a reason behind it, but it's up to us to listen to him. Maybe he is just trying to get our attention. I do not know, but I'm praying.

Dominica will get back on its feet, that is for sure. Dominica is a blessed nation. We are receiving help from all around the world. It's so nice to see a nation and the world in general pulling together to help another. Too much fighting. I appreciate the union even if it is for a short period. I do hope that all is well with you. One day we will finally meet to have lunch or something like that. Have yourself a blessed day.

September 4, 2015

Stein

Good day to you.

It is just about 6:19 as I write this note to you. Occurred to me as I did my morning "chant a psalm a day" that I should send you the verse that caught my attention and my reflections.

It came from 2 Timothy 1, where Paul says, "For God did not give us a spirit of timidity (of cowardice, of craven and cringing and fawning fear), but [He has given us a spirit] of power and of love and of calm and well-balanced mind and discipline and self-control." Spirit of power and love, of sound mind, calm, and this dwells in you and me, in us.

Often, I think of this awesome power at the base of my belly, truly throughout my blood, bones, nervous system as energy, moving me on. I control nothing under my skin! How magnificent it is to speak about myself as if separate from that which gives me life, and even when I think as man that I have my own thoughts, even when I reflect on the power of the Holy Spirit active in me, the breath of life lives in me.

I can say I do not believe in God, but to say that, I need language or thought, and neither of these is possible without breath. I thank God that I am familiar with this and look to it for my sustenance.

And even as I say this, I am aware that simply to think this is the Spirit at work in me, thinking thoughts that I call my thoughts but which I myself do not produce. I do not know the origin of thought, memory, dreams, visions. They arise in me.

They arise in you too. Think of yourself standing, sitting, full of life, having given life. Everything about you is yours, given to you. Hey, it has even been given a name! But truly, who is it? What is it that lives in you, that moves you to thought and action, having constituted you to stand, run, talk, gesticulate, hold, love your child, and more? Too heavy for Friday morning.

What are you eating today? Where did it come from? How it nourishes you!

Your partner,

—Stein

Sent this article to Jolita, one written by Zara Barrie. Zara Barrie is a senior writer for Elite Daily. Elite Daily describes Zara as woman consumed by style, sexuality, women, words, fashion, and feelings. The article is titled "Me, Myself And I: 9 Divine Qualities of a Badass Babe Who Goes Out by Herself." It reads:

There is just something so wildly magnetic about a badass babe who dares to go out by herself. Not with a date. Not in a sea of girls hungry to meet fresh boy blood.

I'm talking about the intriguing, one-of-a-kind VIXEN who takes herself out on glorious dates. She teems with mystery. She's an undeniable force in which to be reckoned with. She's different from the rest.

She's got a style that can't be carbon-copied. She's refreshingly chic, impossibly glamorous, yet has playful prowess that's lightyears ahead of her time. She's one of a kind. She is sexy because she radiates a fierce independence that is palpable, almost electric to every entity tucked into the bar. Her naturally rebellious energy infatuates the masses, for every single soul in sight is collectively curious about who this fascinating and elusive girl-creature is.

She's the sort of girl who simply likes herself enough to treat herself. She's a fearless style rebel, the kind of girl who smashes the boring fashion "rules" with her nail polish-adorned hands.

She's the rare breed who can simultaneously rock a bold lip with an in-your-face smoky eye and actually pull it off. Though she oozes inherent charm, she's not here to impress you. In fact, she doesn't need anyone besides her awesome self.

She's privy to the most important secret that takes too many girls too long to learn: You are the best friend you will ever have. She likes herself enough to treat herself.

She takes herself out on the town while leaving the rest of the population lost in universal wonder. A plethora of eyes watch her; they are hyper inquisitive, ravenous to know more about this mysterious vamp. For there are divine qualities exclusive to the badass babe who dares to venture out alone:

She's Brimming With Confidence
While there are a surplus of girls scattered around the city whose confidence is directly reliant on the number of attractive bodies they

surround themselves with, the girl who dines alone is not one of these girls.

Again, she's just not like most people. She attains a unique confidence, the kind that comes from deep within herself, not from the validation of others.

While she's a wildly social creature, when faced with the choice, she would prefer to bask in her own fierce company than heaps of fake friends and meaningless acquaintances. She's A Girl Who Sets Trends, Doesn't Follow Them, A girl who is fierce enough to go out by herself is fierce enough to own her personal style. She doesn't read fashion magazines to discover what she should wear; she is inspired by the world around her. She's a creative individual who garners her inspiration from the fabulous displays of street-style she observes from countries across the globe. She is inspired by an international crew of other badass babes who boldly express themselves; yet, she always makes it her own. If she likes something, she fearlessly wears it with reckless abandon. She plays and experiments with style; there is no set formula to her look.

Subsequently, she becomes the girl who sets the trends, not the one who follows them. Her authentic style intrigues girls everywhere, and they all attempt to emulate her fresh aesthetic. She's The Modern-Day Vixen While the girl who goes out by herself is most definitely a modern woman who unabashedly thrives in the modern world, she also has the unexpected classic glamour of the Hollywood screen siren.

In this age of incessant over-sharing, the badass babe provides us with a much-needed smattering of mystique. There is just something so fascinating and seductive about an independent girl all dressed up, indulging in her own company at the bar. She's simply a rare vixen. She's An Empowered Feline.

So when observing a mysterious, mega babe, who is blissfully by herself, we can't help but feel a sweeping sensation of ferocious admiration. After all, is there a single more empowering thing for a woman to do than take herself out? By getting dressed to the nines in the attire she adores and treating herself to a night out, she's declaring to the universe that she's worthy of her own company. She Has Her Own Set of Rules Society is forever telling us girls that a night out on the town is an activity reserved for dates or in the company of a large group of friends. The girl who rebels against this dated notion is a girl who challenges the system. She doesn't subscribe to the oppressive rules. The only rules she answer's to are the ones she sets for her badass self. She's Beautifully Adventurous. One of the great lures to going out, in general, is not knowing what fascinating entity you just might meet. But all too often we go out in big, massive groups and only engage with people we already know. This is absolutely NOT the case for the badass babe who goes out alone. Because she's not caught up in a sea of familiar faces, and instead has opted to fly solo. She has opened herself up to meeting other beautifully adventurous free spirits who are daring enough to explore the world alone. She's A Free Bird.

The girl alone at the bar is FREE. She's not attached to her boyfriend. She's not co-dependent on her friends. She doesn't need to be shackled to the plans of others in order to feel secure.

She does what she wants, when she wants and is always ready for the night to take an unexpected, exciting turn. She Has Killer Instincts.

A girl who is so impressively independent, so authentically rebellious and so gorgeously self-assured; is a girl who listens to her gut. She's in touch with her instincts. She doesn't need anyone else to tell her what's right or what's wrong. She boldly listens to her intuition. She doesn't question the voice within her, so she is always, always safe. She's A Glamorous Badass.

The girl alone at the bar is a real badass. A real badass is a different breed than the false "badass" mean girls who use cheap intimidation tactics to scare off the masses. A real badass is a ferocious chick who thinks for herself. It's the girl who fearlessly speaks her gorgeous mind. It's the lady that knows what she likes.

She's the girl who doesn't require compliments to sustain her self-esteem. She's the girl who dresses for herself. She's a rebel. She's wild, untamable and gloriously playful.

https://www. elitedaily.com/life/9-divine-qualitiesbadass-babe-goes/1117021 last visited September 3, 2015

September 4, 2015

Jolita

Hi,

This is a beautiful piece. That's the description of a very beautiful woman—bold and Beautiful. That's very rare in today's society.

Women are so caught up with the things around them. They want to do, dress, and act like what they see in magazines, TV, and all other social media. No one dares to be themselves, to stand out, to make a statement by the way they live their life. Everyone is afraid of what others may say or think. We do not rely on our instinct; we are afraid it may show our true selves. What we do not realize is that our true selves is what describes us, what makes us stand out. We can never truly find ourselves if we keep pretending to be someone else—pretending to be others just so that we can please fake friends.

You can never truly have a real friend or be a real friend if that person doesn't really know that real you. We need to learn to be yourself; act out a little, be a rebel when you feel in the mood. Let not your friends or that eye candy disturb you from being you. The true you will attract the type of friends that you need around you. Not everyone will like you for you, but who cares? You need to love you—love you for who you are, the way you are, and feel comfortable.

I am not too bold about it, but I love me, I do me. I will act out when I feel like it. I just don't care most times. When I do this, I feel free. I feel like me, like I can do anything, and nothing anyone may say will bring me down. Other times, I admit I pay special attention to what I wear and the way I act, cause' I can really draw too much attention, and I can't always stand it. So I hide me and act like the crowd. Blend in. It's not that much of a bad thing, I believe.

I do hope that you do you. You be you, no matter what. Nothing is worth losing you over. Be Stein. He's the greatest. Love him!

On Friday September 11, 2015, I sent Jolita two hours of Salsa after she surprised me with a call from her Magic Jack. It was 7:25 a.m. and she was at work. She informed me that she's usually at work early. I was delighted to hear Jolita. She wrote back that Friday.

Thank you, I love it.

It was so nice talking to you this morning, hearing your voice again. It is just so enriching every time I talk to you. You always put a smile on my face— had me bubbly for the whole day. Can't wait to hear from you again and learn the art of meditation. Hope you are having a great day.

Love,

J.

September 14, 2015

Stein

Remembered working along with Madonna and the album *Ray of Light* in the background. It's rare, beautiful listening. Used it while I worked. It's gentle and nonobtrusive.

Otherwise, it's just cool, thick, even dark, sensual, provocative, hidden, mysterious, like someone.

I'm getting to know…

Love,

St.

September 14, 2015

Jolita

Beautiful! I like it.

You were on the radio this morning? I heard a voice it sounded like yours.

Hope you are having a good day today.

September 15, 2015

Stein

Where are you reading my note and receiving my songs from? Thought your staff were asked to stay home in view of a flood watch and tropical wave. Felt like talking with you this morning…

Hmmm. You have an ear and taste for music. I understand when a person says I have an ear for music, but I never understand the "taste" for music. Taste transcends the tongue, I suppose. I gather consumers these days do not only consume food, but cars, TV sets, iPhones, etc.

Wow, a taste for music you have…

Hoping you're having a great day too.

—St.

Jolita wrote back:

I was reading from by my mom. That is as far as I got that morning. I stayed there a bit with my son. I heard the voice, and I swear I was listening to you.

I couldn't call you back—my boyfriend hates the way I sound on the phone. He is threatened by my speech. He believes that I sound a lot like I'm flirting, and it's disturbing to our relationship, so I try my best not to answer or have any conversations when he is around. I am so sorry. I got to work late this morning. That's why I did not call you.

I love music that touches the heart. I am not sure that I understand the concept of tasting music, but I guess that when you are so much into the music, you hear it, you feel it, it's like you almost want to live it.

Then I guess at that point, all that's left to do is taste it!

How have you been for the past time? I must say I miss hearing your voice.

Have yourself a blessed day today.

—J.

September 16, 2015

Stein

Yes, it was me you heard. I enjoy discussions regarding the psychological and psychiatric, and whenever it arises in Dominica or elsewhere, I listen and, on occasions, participate.

Must be one of my old encounters—I used to teach sociology to psychiatric nurses at Princess Margaret Hospital (Dominica).

Hope you're well, J. You are in Dominica, and though you may not have been directly affected by floods, a collective sense of loss pervades the society—it can even be felt over distance by those Dominicans living in the diaspora. It's an excellent time to listen…

I've covered some 120 pages of the 207 that I'm editing for this lady in Houston. She's Dominican, and her story touches the subject of depression and her struggles with it. Riveting narrative.

So I'm at work, though this morning I stopped a while for a long meditation. Didn't sleep quietly last night. Thing is, I tried something. I attempted to sleep on my back. I usually sleep on my belly or sides. Whenever I sleep on my back, I tend to time-travel, meditate, or just travel to other worlds. It is a sort of letting go. Don't know if you ever tried it. Pretty interesting and brave too.

There's so much I would like to tell you for your own good and development, and of course, as one goes through life, things, issues arise. Roses come with thorns. Think of it, Dominica has water all around and in it, but people cannot have water to drink. It is a grand paradox…

As long as you arrive early at work, call me. I am at my station from 4:30 a.m. till 2:00 p.m.

Thoughts of you came to mind with regard to the song "Substitute for Love" by Madonna. Heard you humming it. I like "Power of Goodbye."

Love.

September 16, 2015

Jolita

Good day, Stein,

Ah, I know that I knew that voice. I was convinced it was you. I think they need to put you back on radio! That voice needs to be heard, and you have a lot of helpful and informative things to say.

I rarely get time to listen to the radio—well, I think I actually don't make the time. My father is always listening to Q-95, and I just can't take in any more politics. It is absolutely too much for me now. Found myself listening to Kairi, and the discussion at that point just caught my ears. I like listening to information that is going to teach me something, enlighten my thinking, and in turn, put me to think. It was a good discussion. Should have been longer. I believe that there was more that could have been said. It was so great. The levels and studies that you have gone through in your life, I am so amazed. I want to be like that. After this year, I want to be more knowledgeable in the fields of sociology, psychology, politics, and anything else that takes my attention. I have to do some studies just for my own benefit, and so I could talk with you more on other issues. Doing some conversational English might help. It is a tragic situation that Dominica has been faced with—families and friends lost, homes and properties gone. I wasn't directly affected but still affected. I love rain, and now, the slightest change of weather has me on edge thinking about my family, friends, coworkers, and even the people I meet on a day-to-day basis. The hurt, the fear. It is a lot. It is too much right now. Dominica will rise again, but it will never be the same. How will the families that have lost everything get back up and start all over? It is going to be very difficult for them.

The conditions in which they are living right now are not the best. My heart cries out for them and for Dominica on a whole. I cannot properly imagine how it is to have been going through that.

After so many years on this Earth, I have never seen, nor have I ever thought I would see such a thing in this island. I can't imagine the hurt and pain.

Dominica has been spared from so many bad weathers in the past; we were a blessed nation. Wonder if that is still true. Some say it's a purification of the land that is taking place, but I don't know. All I can say is that God giveth and he taketh away. He has his reasoning for all he does. He doesn't have to answer to me or anyone. He knows what he is doing, and I trust him through it all. Come high waters, come floods, he is in control. I will not understand why he does what he does, but I trust him. As this song says, "And the God of the mountain is still God in the valley / When things go wrong, he'll make them right / And the God of the good time is still God in the bad times / And the God of the Day is still God in the night." Through it all, he was still there.

I will call you in the mornings. We still have our meditation to do. I really want to try it. Trying to sleep on my back doesn't work. I am never really sleeping, and my mind keeps going all night. I can no longer just think of a topic or thing and concentrate on it. The mind goes and goes about everything. My mind is never at rest, and that can be so disturbing at times. I need that moment of stillness just to rest the mind before it runs me to the psychiatric unit. I just think too much at times, and it's crazy. It gets me in trouble 'cause I sometimes end up saying out what I am thinking. I need a mind break, or as you put it, I need to let go.

Well, concentrate on your work. You still got a few pages to run through. Maybe one day I'll write my own book or get a book written about me. Ha-ha!

How do you know I'd be humming that song today? I listened to it a lot yesterday. It is so heart-touching, so sensual; it almost made me believe that I was in need of a substitute for love. It's a song to make a lonely heart go searching for a taste of a substitute for love. Just thinking of this song already got me so excited. I love this song.

Enjoy your day today. Hoping to speak to you in the morning.

September 21, 2015

Stein

Good day to you.

Uncovered these songs from Indian singer Noor Jehan. I do not understand the lyrics, but the emotion, the beat as they progress ...

Don't know if this tallies with your "search sensibility" into other cultures, but I cared to give it a try, send it to you. Today, I celebrate my birthday and went in search of great persons born September 21 from ancient times to these times. Then I selected all the composers born on September 21, and Noor Jehan was one of the greats: https://www.youtube.com/watch?v=6YOzKN3L27w.

Sept. 21, 2015

Jolita

Happy birthday to you,

Happy birthday to you,

Happy birthday, dear Stein,

Happy birthday to you.

You're just six years old now

You're just six years old now

Enjoy it while you are still young

Age is creeping with sound

Happy birthday!

I wish you a blessed birthday today, and may you see so many more years to come. I wish you life, health, wealth, and sight to see beyond the normal today. It is not every day you get to be 06. Love it, embrace it. It should be a joy to go through all the journeys you went through in life and live up to this point in life where you can look back and say, "I have lived a life, but I'm not done yet." Still young, full of energy, and most importantly, you have life. You have reached the age that most young people today may never have the chance to reach. Wish I was there to spend it with you. Enjoy it.

I don't understand how this life works. You are not getting old at all. You are just increasing in numbers. You don't look a day over thirty. Keep doing what you are doing. Take care of you and stop counting age so I could meet up to your age someday soon. Ha-ha! Enjoy the day!

September 21, 2015

Stein

It happened one day. She called to find specifics, and we fell in a moment I shall not name. We took to speaking, sharing silences, moments of discomfort over our immediate synchrony, and this would not be the end. No, we would spend remaining weeks longing to share words, breaths, silences again, and we did one magnificent day, her tender tone practically girlish parity to innocence juxtaposed in dark thick- ness. She called me to say she was ready for me ready to speak with me, and when she left, I was empty, drained, thirsting thus. When she writes to wish me happy birthday, she recaptures remembrances, unspoken desire, wishes too early, too separate to call out, too normative, too shy to utter. He knows she knows the fire is mutual.

—S da Silva Henry

September 22, 2015

Jolita

Good day,

This is a very beautiful piece. I love it. Got me smiling, actually laughing for the day. How was the birthday? What else did you do for the day? Can't wait to hear from you, seeing you know me too well.

September 23, 2015

Stein

Spent the morning looking through names of great persons in history born on September 21. Well, I found many dating back to the fourteenth century.

As I told you, I excerpted all composers of music and took to listening to bits of their work in search of something I could relate to, given our similar birth date.

That took up most of my morning into early afternoon until my wife came home and I fell asleep with her. She usually rests after coming from work.

Must tell you, though, that the party is this weekend. How did this come to be? Well, historically, I've celebrated my birthday until September 23 under the belief borrowed from my father that I was really supposed to have been born on September 23, but my mother was a bit busy!

Be that as it may, there is a woman who works in hospital medicine at Atlanta's main hospital—Emory. We speak. She's a family friend. She was telling me two weeks ago that her birthday is coming up soon, and she did not know what she was going to do. I asked about the date, and she said September 22. So I screamed out. She said, "No, don't tell me your birthday is the same." Now that is against the background that we've been speaking for about two years and do not know when either of us was born. When I told her, it was September 21, she suggested that our families have a joint party! We're holding that this weekend! The party continues!

And since our daughter had planned something for her mother and I to mark my birthday, long before our family nurse friend discovered that our birthdays were close and we were both Virgos with touches of Libra, we had to respond to our daughter's call. She had planned a massage and night out for her mother and father to mark my 06th birthday. Ha-ha. Well, that will be on the following weekend. My celebrations are likely to run into October, as the old people say, God willing!

I must say, I reread the poem, and even to me who wrote it, it is real cool, beautiful—a quality of enchantment. I don't know what we will say when we meet each other. Often I wonder if we like each other only from a distance... I doubt.

I do not know you well. I think you know yourself well, and I know myself well. And I am not even sure about either. We create a new dimension when our two selves meet, each knowing itself. Hmmm.

You asked me to do Stein. Just imagine "thick" meets "slender." My lord!

Much love to you.

—St.

September 25, 2015

Jolita

Hello, hello, hello. It has been a while. I am truly sorry. Got myself overwhelmed with work issues, home, and most of all, planning my sister's wedding. It has just been a busy week.

You are not a September 23 born, and don't blame your mom. It was you who were too busy to see the world. She couldn't even walk because of you. You fought your way out, and when you got to the part where it was just too difficult and complicated, you tried to turn back, but at that time, it was way too late. She pushed you out as hard as she could.

You almost killed the lady. You tore that pink flesh right down the middle. The little scars can still be seen today!

You can take your mind off this right now. You are going to think about this too in-depth. It's your birthday month. Enjoy it. Free up yourself, have a drink, but not more than two. September is almost over. October is not yours to take. Enjoy the rest of your month. Party, dance, scream. You are younger than you have been in so many years. Don't forget to finish editing the book, though.

I like being in our little dimension. It is so eye-opening and enhancing. It has always been my pleasure to talk to you. You are more than entertaining, well informed, and that personality is to die for, as the young people would say. Enjoy the balance of your day. Hoping to speak to you soon.

Love,

J.

Ms. Thick (Ha-ha!)

October 13, 2015

Stein

Good day to you. Just in case you are interested and find time, you should read this attached judgment of the Privy Council regarding the case of *Lennox Linton v. Kieron Pinard-Byrne*.

I don't think this morning's conversation requires any further comment.

Love.

October 20, 2015

Jolita

How are you doing today? I haven't called yet. It has been a lil busy on my end here. But I will try my best to hear your voice before this week ends. Missing our conversations. My morning smiles. Continuing to thank God every time I remember you. Have a blessed day today.

Love,

J.

November 27, 2015

Stein

I have tried on several occasions to contact you by telephone, but without success. How are you? I understood from one gentleman at your workplace that you were on leave. I wondered why you did not just drop me a note to let me know you would be out so I would not have to try to find you.

It has been quite a while since I read you, and I sure hope you can drop another line. If circumstances make it difficult or if there was something I said or wrote that displeased you, I hope those sentiments are temporary. Just in case you do not write back, I want to say it was a pleasure communicating with you. God bless.

—St.

December 2, 2015

Jolita

Good morning,

I am back. I am so sorry I didn't inform you that I would have been out. I needed a break from this place—a short break but a break nonetheless. I am great, needing more rest 'cause it really wasn't rest, but I am good.

How are you doing? Hoping that the natural healing process is working great for you. How is the family? How is Stein? Tell me what has been going on with you lately.

Love,

J.

December 7, 2015

Jolita

Hi.

Good day, Stein,

It was very nice hearing your voice. Oh gosh, you always lighten up my day. Just the slightest thought of you makes my day seem more than possible. The most stressful of days seem at ease with the sweet sound of your voice touching my ear in the morning.

I know I am blessed to have a friend like you. You make life seem so simple and perfect. Time seems to slow down just enough to make the day perfect. Thank you. Have yourself a blessed day today. Happy Monday.

Love,

J.

I thank God every time I think of you!

December 8, 2015

Stein

It seemed a long time since I had not heard from you by way of writing. Even though I write, I find delight in reading your pulses.

Your energy and emotions are so evident in your words and tender yet disciplined voice. You sound alert and in rhythm.

I thank God every time I think of you.

Love,

S.

December 9, 2015

Stein

Thought of you today. Even attempted to call you, touch base with your effervescence and smile. I sensed today was full, and you, knowing you apply yourself to the work at hand, would be busy multitasking.

This text is slipping into touching. It needs to stay at the level of criminal law. Remember that initial, that original oeuvre...

Must find you a song for inclusion in my next mail. Today I read Derek Walcott writing in the poem "Parang"-"flesh upon flesh was the tune since the first cloud raise up to disclose the breast of the naked moon."

I breathed in to learn this inherent mystery.

Love to you.

—St.

December 10, 2015

Jolita

Good morning,

You read very interesting poems. That simple line excited my morning a bit too much this morning. I kept rereading this line, putting myself in the position, trying to feel the intensity of this situation, fantasizing on the passion and fire between these two flesh. Oh gosh, the hunger, the yearning! This seems too intense, too emotional. The criminality in this situation is at a high. I do believe for this case to be properly judged, it needs to be evaluated at a different angle. I believe the situation needs to be relived and properly examined. The nature of this case calls for such things. Reading this case entices a lust that needs to go further than just in the mind of the listener, it needs to be felt.

I am going to leave it at that and return to work! It's always a pleasure hearing from you. Have a good day.

Love,

J.

December 16, 2015

Jolita

Good morning,

Just thought I would say hi.

How are you doing? How's the family? Can you see me any clearer today? I do hope the natural healing process is doing good for you.

Hoping to read a piece from you soon. Have yourself a good day.

Love,

J.

December 16, 2015

Stein

You must've written this note just as I was coming out of my meditation. Thanks for your kind words and thoughtfulness. Not too cheerful this morning, though I am quite strong and giving thanks. I find too many of my friends are not being friendly.

Maybe it's the time of year. Maybe I think too much about those I love, care about, and pray for. I find myself sometimes in deep sorrow over the behavior of my own relatives and friends.

My immediate family is fine, though I think, with the cold weather approaching even more, days get heavier and people silenter. Winter is wonderful when it is celebrated, but I don't think this celebratory practice is part of Georgia's culture. Remember too, that I lived among Canadians for five years, and they, they have a totally different view of winter. There, it's cold and is cause for reflection, great reading, home conversation, warm blankets, thick stockings, great coffee, porridges, soups.

As for my sight and natural healing, I am convinced that a miracle is unfolding in my life and eyes. As a result, I enter periods of sharp negativity, and though fragmentary, they tell me that something's shifting. Herbs and plants are effective, but I am discovering that my mind state and spiritual health/ well-being are key to this unfolding. Then of course, it is going to happen the seeing, that is, just at the point when I least expect. I may just find I'm running down the stairs. So much for grace!

I'm heavy this morning, and I need to hear your voice, but you will not call me, and when I call you I do not find you. I'm sensitive...How's your son and your lover? You must be in paradise. Remember me.

I hope I have the opportunity to speak with you, at the very least, to wish you Christmas some- thing and a new year full of everything.

Love.

December 28, 2015

Stein

What has happened to you, girl? I don't hear from you anymore. Did I say something wrong? No Christmas greetings, no bells, no jingles, no angel wishes. I gather the New Year must be bringing light to you. And for this, I give thanks.

Love,

S.

December 31, 2015

Jolita

Merry Christmas, Happy New Year, and I wish you the best for the year. It has been such a busy end of year. Not even your messages I'm having time to read. I'm sorry, but I thank God it's over and I am still alive and well. He has surely seen me through a lot. I am still here and still sane. Christmas was great. Enjoyed it with the family, cousins, aunts, uncles. That is what my Christmas was like, and I loved it. There is no better feeling than being around the ones I love for Christmas. Missed my Stein, though.

How are you? How was the Christmas for you? Hope you saved me some fruit cake and rum punch or whatever people in your part of the States eat for Christmas.

Love,

J.

December 31, 2015

Stein

Wines, sorrel, ginger-beer, fruitcake, rum cake, orange cake, green tea cake, grain breads, coconut cakes, hams, chicken, shrimp, crabs, spinach, cucumbers, cabbages, colored greens, kale, tomatoes, ginger, turmeric, rosemary, blueberries, strawberries, mixed nuts, peanuts, cashew, grafted oranges, chocolates, pomegranates, beers, plantains, yams, cassava, pears, papaya, cantaloupe, apples, coconut milk, lettuce, bananas, and more and sometimes nothing, just nothing.

January 12, 2016

Jolita

How are you? It is such a beautiful day today! Lovely weather, hot sun, but thank God for air-conditioned buildings: I'm cool. There isn't supposed to be rain today, but I am praying for a little bit just to cool down this heat tonight. Oh, how I miss talking to you! You always have some great insights on life. It is always a pleasure reading from you. Oh, how I miss my Stein. Your messages just send a tingle through me. I really do need to write more. I think I am getting writer's block. I have no more words. I don't know what to say anymore. I just know that I need to say something. How is the New Year treating you, my friend? How is the family?

January 13, 2016

Stein

The year is new, the soul is old, ancient being living under our skin. You've been chosen to be my writing partner, and if I have to scream to draw this to your attention, I will. There's no woman who has written to me as profusely as you've done and so intuitively, over the last year. Moreover, in the last ten years, I have not had a flow of letters (do we still call them letters) from anyone. This may not serve to justify my claim before a hopeful attorney-at-law, but this is truth.

I am aware of what you're feeling. It's called an effulgence—a sort of emergent flow that sometimes overwhelms. And true to source, you say it's a writer's block. Well blockages hold back, build up, and finally break.

Can't wait to read the flow. You write well.

When we Skype and I gather we can speak for longer periods and you, away from work—I will tell you how much your writings inspire. You should continue to record your thoughts-so sharp, so pregnant! Woosssh! I didn't mean that!

I look forward to our conversation, my friend (as you call me). Friendship must be quite special to you. As I must've told you before, your friend is your needs answered. I read this from Kahlil Gibran, the Lebanese poet.

To tell you about the new year is to tell you about my grandson, my son's son. I went to the bath- room to pee. He, the four-year old, followed me. He stood watching me, and when I was through, he said in that most instructive voice, "Papa, wash your hands." He had learned this at day care. On another occasion, I took to massaging the lower parts of his body-thighs, feet, and toes. He was quite jumpy as my fingers probed him. When the massage was over, he went to his grandmother and said, "Papa stretched my toes." When he got home to Jacksonville, he told his mother the same stretched-my-toes story. While she was speaking with me, I heard him in the back- ground, "Happy New Year, Papa." Out of the mouths of babes and sucklings...

The eleven-month old is a fabulous mix. He has been teething, and of course, once the children get into day care here, it's infection after infection. The eczema is gone 99 percent-a spot or three still remains. He still has a cough, but this has improved tremendously over the last four weeks. He still has a slight diaper itch. Imagine me, sight limited, creeping behind him as he crawls through the alley! I've stopped writing. My logical brain is on sabbatical. I am into random flow, illogical yet wise. This is the child. My wife spent the Christmas making cakes. Every Christmas she receives orders facilitated by our daughter in part and through her own efforts. Our house has this permanent aroma of something cooking or baking. Yet I am slender. Well, so much for metabolism and the power of attraction inherent in that which is slender and that which is thick!

Think I've broken rules and lines of demarcation, though you never stated and we never agreed on rules of discourse. But I must tell you, I am well, listening, meditating, writing a bit but not as abundantly as I would like. Calypsos are indeed intriguing, but sometimes I find the melodies recycled. Still, we love calypso -- there's always one that catches our attention. Love "Shadow Flow!" From here, this flow could go on forever.

Love.

January 13, 2015
Jolita

Oh gosh, you have me giggling away at my desk. It's amusing to me the behaviors and ways of the little ones growing up. It's so fascinating that this once little baby that is supposed to take instructions finds himself giving instructions instead. Showing off what he once learnt and hopefully is practicing. That's just so sweet. It is these sweet moments that last a lifetime. These are the times that we as parents cherish: the giggles, the laughs, the rude interruption just to get your attention, their vivid imagination, and the way in which they retain things and study everything around them. It's just amazing and scary how much kids today pick up. I'm praying for my son every day because there is so much in the environment, and kids tend to pull more to the negative. Oh, how I love him!

I swear if I didn't know you had a problem with your eyes. I would never be able to pick that up through your writing. I swear you see things too clearly. I am jealous of your grandson. Maybe one day I will have to visit for a massage too!

You sound like this Christmas was extra wonderful. Having your grandchildren around just made it more enjoyable. I am one to enjoy that time of year just for the togetherness, the bonding. I think that is what it is all about. Oh, it is also about the food, but I am not a food person, so it's about the family to me. It was so nice hearing your voice yesterday. My Skype will be downloaded today, so I'll be able to hear your voice again later.

For now, have yourself a blessed day.

Love,

J.

January 14, 2016

Stein

Good day, beloved. Do smart work today.

—St.

January 14, 2016

Jolita

Are you okay? Is everything all right?

January 14, 2016

Jolita

Hope you had a wonderful day today, and I pray that it gets better as the day winds down. Love, J.

Jan 15, 2016

Stein

Didn't realize you were such a sensitive woman. You follow patterns-true traits of a criminal lawyer, though in this case the crime is love and the punishment is more love. You were able to spot immediately a change in the tone of my letter. Not only was it short, I gather you "heard" something else in the few words. But as you stated, it was the brevity which caught your attention.

Like my father would say, "There's nothing unusual out here." It was just one of those mornings when I needed to say something to you, but the words would not flow. They shouted from their rebellion post, their refusal to surface—go look for her instead. Find her in the physical. Go look for her.

I asked them to bear with me. She's so forthright and passionate. I needed to prepare myself for that encounter in which half of me saw and the other touched. I could only imagine her sense of touch, and because of the nature of touch and its absence of words, I did not want her to describe hers, yet if she did, I would melt and stand again. Love.

January 15, 2016

Jolita

Hello,

There are many sides of me that are not yet discovered. Search a little deeper and you will find too many sides, too little time.

When I find a good friend, I pay close attention. I need to make sure you are you and spot when something seems different in you. It's also shocking to know that your words would not flow. You are a man of many meaningful words, words to encourage, words to touch, words to uplift, and words that put a smile on my face.

You have a way with words like none other. Your words know just how much to melt a woman, just so that you could scoop her up again. I can just imagine you saying those words to me, so breathtaking. Hope you are having yourself a great day.

Love, J.

January 15, 2016

Stein

I do not think the blockage activity was in effect an inhibition as much as an opportunity to acknowledge amazement and also to press on from that fragment of thought that remained open to me.

Had a weird thought this morning. You know things come into our minds without our asking, like a song that comes in and stays a day. I took to thinking, what if she's showing what I write to anyone. It had never occurred before. In the interest of transparency, I thought I'd mention it. I treat your communication as precious and worthy for reflection.

It's Friday, and communication from you is real nice—at least I have some thought to roll on with till you surface again Monday. Hope you had a productive week.

Two days ago, I felt a slight itch in my throat, only to discover today that I have traces of a flu. This is normal in winter, though I have not had flu in years. In fact, apart from my sight limitation, I am seldom sick, and I give thanks.

So you can well imagine the counsel I am receiving from those who call and hear the slight husky tone in my voice-drink this and drink that. Well, if they're Dominican, you're sure to hear lime and honey, and if it is an older woman, it is gargle with warm saltwater. Then the more experimental ones would suggest throwing in a bit of garlic. It is all good, they say. I settle for squeezed lemon and warm water, take to resting a bit longer and intensifying my meditation and bicycle sweat. But these simply strengthen -- a flu has to run its course.

It's 36 degrees Fahrenheit out here in Stone Mountain, just outside Atlanta. There's rain too... makes for excellent sleep.

Your reflection on my text is lucid, passionate, and pure. You would have to be sure about your feelings to speak so frankly to me. You would have to want to.

You write, "I can just imagine you saying those words to me, so breathtaking." This is cyber girl and Google is gonna give our communication to the Thought Police (LOL). Let's be cool here. This Friday, and each Friday we agree to summarize emotions, create synopses of our feelings that baffle those who would care to peep.

Intriguing adventure.

Truth is, Friday's note can always be long. It is only natural that it is since we seek to make up for the weekend absence and our love for communicating. As we stated earlier on, some things are just not for text and song. Remember Walcott in the poem "Parang," when he wrote, "Flesh on flesh was the tune." It just has to be felt. You responded. Wow! Great weekend... Love

January 21, 2016

Jolita

Good morning,

Oh my. You must think I have forgotten you. Please note that I have not forgotten you. It is a bit busy here on my end, trying to catch up with the work for the month and see its completion. I must say I am halfway there and will get to the end before the month end, God willing. Please note that what we say here is only between us two. I would never show out what has been said here. It is for our eyes only to read because no one else would be able to understand the passion through these words.

I hope you have already gotten rid of this flu. Its course should be over by now. Try not to get it again. With this weather you have up there, this flu might be lingering around, but please if it is, inform it that its due date has passed, passport expired-time for the flu to move on. I myself seem to be getting a flu, but it's not too bad yet.

Trying to get rid of it before it gets worse. I hate the flu.

How is your grandson doing? How is the editing going? I was just thinking about life, how things work out so strangely. You never thought you would be here today. I am just wondering in the next twenty years, where will I be? Who will I be? How will I be? Will I still be here? The future is changing no matter how we try, we can't stop what is to happen. It is said that we shape our own futures, we choose our own paths, but I don't believe that it is all up to us. We try our best, but if it is not part of God's plan, then no matter what steps we take to bring us where we want to be, it will not work. Barriers and limitations that is a sign. Some we can overcome. Others are just there to direct us to the path we need to be on. Your barriers directed you to places and things you never expected, and every time a door of opportunity would close on you, a better door opens. When your sight started to give up, I know that frightened you. What would you do? How would you go on if you couldn't see? But here you are able to read what I am writing and communicating with me so well.

Hope you are having a good evening.

Love, J.

January 21, 2016

(Call and Response)

Jolita: Good morning.

Stein: Good afternoon to you..... so happy to read you.

Jolita: Stein, oh my. You must think I have forgotten you. Please note that I have not forgotten you.

Stein: I never think of you forgetting me because frequently I remember you in any one day. One guy ran a line by a woman. He said to her, "You are always running through my mind." She told him that that was such an old line. It is not possible to always think of someone-the mind does not work that way. But as for forgetting, I never forget you because you have become integral to my thoughts ... I do not forget. Neither do I always remember. You come and go at will......

Jolita: Busy here on my end trying to catch up with the work for the month and see its completion. I must say I am halfway there and will get to the end before month end, God willing.

Stein:Good luck. You stay focused anyway.

Jolita: **Stein,** please note that what we say here is only between us two. I would never show out what has been said here. It is for our eyes only to read because no one else would be able to understand the passion through these words.

Stein: I am happy you recognize passion in our words. I wish these were the days when people wrote letters with ink and paper, at least for its privacy. It could be an excellent debate- -comparing the safety of letter-writing with pen and paper and the post and, today writing and hitting Enter/ Ctrl or clicking Send. When you speak too, as a means of communication, your voice is so sweet to my ears, so sensual, so allowing. I feel like I want to just let you hold me while you speak whatever comes to mind-a free flow of feelings, an act of disappearing languages, a curled lip, gentle breathing. Hmmm!

Jolita: I hope you have already gotten rid of this flu. Its course should be over by now. Try not to get it again. With this weather you have up there, this flu might be lingering around, but please, if it is, inform it that it's due date has passed, passport expired, time for the flu to move on. I myself seem to be getting a flu, but it's not too bad yet-trying to get rid of it before it gets worse. I hate the flu.

Stein: A bit of it is around. It lingers just in the upper regions of my lung, and I want to make sure all the mucus is gone. There's a bit of coughing, but the initial "whoop" is gone. Also, it is still evident in the tone of my voice, a sort of nasal speaking. Fight as best you can since you have a child around and these flus can be so contagious. The sea is such great cure.

Jolita: How is your grandson doing?

Stein: He's happy. Has developed a new laugh and still thinks he must stay up playing at night. We've mixed his care services for a few days of the week, he'll be at day care and the remaining days in private care. He too still carries remains of a cough, but his skin is completely cleared. We give thanks. We're treating and curing what remains of that cough.

Jolita: How is the editing going?

Stein: Wish it were more coherent. I think the weight of reading and researching has caught and held my attention. Remember when I was a teenager, my father kept me reading, and I used to complain how I wanted to go out and do something. He warned that if I had to "do something," I had to read. So I have read by listening, and now my writing has lifted its wings, about to fly from its cinnamon nest. Let's see how the flight unfolds and lands again and flies again. How magnificent it would be if we could write something together!

Jolita: I was just thinking about life, how things work out so strange. You never thought you would be here today. I am just wondering in the next twenty years, where will I be? Who will I be? How will I be? Will I still be here? The future is changing. No matter how we try, we can't stop what is to happen. It is said that we shape our own futures, we choose our own paths, but I don't believe that it is all up to us. We try our best, but if it is not part of God's plan, then no matter what steps we take to bring us where we want to be, it will not work. Barriers and limitations -- that is a sign. Some we can overcome. Others are just there to direct us to the path we need to be on. Your barriers directed you to places and things you never expected, and every time a door of opportunity would close on you, a better door opens. When your sight started to give up, I know that frightened you. What would you do? How would you go on if you couldn't see? But here you are able to read what I am writing and communicating with me so well.

Stein: This passage I hope to deal with in a separate mail. It is a profound one-- think that every branch of hair on your head is counted. You are loved. We shall continue this discussion. Hope you are having a good evening.

January 25, 2016

Stein

I've been thinking about you, and though I have no specific word to pass on, I thought I'd just say hi to you. Hope everything fits well today, from the shoes to your hair. Anything in between carries a sign "trespassers will be prosecuted" except, of course, those who share passionately in the rule-setting fraternity.

It is not as cold here as it had been over the last four days. With movements of that storm Jonas, a trail of cold air remained in its tail- -Stone Mountain plummeted to 10 degrees F. I'm warm, and if you know well, I enjoy cold. The flu still lingers. Seems like it wants to take its own precious time to leave. And it is the way it continues to irritate even as it dissipates. Basically, I am still not completely out of the mountains.

Our little grandson celebrates one year today. We're supposed to go to his parents' house for dinner. I think he spent half the day at day care and was picked up early. Even at this stage, there's a birthday uniform. How was your weekend? When are you setting up the Skype? Let's get going.

I have not yet written the answer to the final paragraph of your last letter. I believe when this is done, it should prove to be revelatory even to me. Be well and take care of yourself.

Love, St.

January 27, 2016
Jolita

Good morning, my dear Stein,

Nothing could fit well on Monday. I am sorry. Took off a wisdom tooth, and thank God the pain is less but not yet gone. I am still waiting for it to heal. My face is still swelling, but by God's grace, I will be all right.

I need you to send some of that cold weather my way. Dominica is getting too hot. I'm turning black down here! Thought you were coming down for the Carnival, listen to some calypso, judge a few shows, parade around in the streets. It is the season, Carnival again.

I am hoping to go see the opening with my son. I'll be waiting for you there.

Have a blessed day.

February 29, 2016
Stein

Hey. Be forever wonderful, be patient, be kind. You are a strong woman, discerning and insightful.

Whatever you choose as your future career or professional interest, make sure you love it, enjoy it, and would be happy to wake each day to engage it.

Whenever you find the time, drop a line. It is always a pleasure to hear from you, to feel the passion in your words. Love now.

March 3, 2016
Jolita

Good day, my dear Stein,

How are you? Oh, how I miss our sweet conversations. Your messages always have a way of tickling my soul.

I am at work now just trying to clear out a backlog of stuff. Can't wait to actually meet you face-to-face. You are an extraordinary person. Have yourself a blessed day.

Love, J.

March 30, 2016

Jolita

Good morning, my dear Stein,

How are you doing? I miss our conversations. How is the healing process going? Natural healing? I believe that we have corrupted our bodies so much over the years and pumped so much artificial medicines in it that it has lost the ability to heal itself from the simplest of things. The body has become so dependent that it struggles now to stand independently.

I do hope for the best for you, even if you may not be able to see clearly as I do. I know that your sight is much greater than that of an ordinary man. You see through eyes that we don't even see.

How are the grands, your bundles of joy? When are you coming to visit us, so we can finally see face-to-face, or something like that.

Have yourself an amazing day. You are an amazing person, and I am thankful for your presence in my life.

Love, J.

March 30, 2016

Stein

You're absolutely correct so much has been put into the body, so much has been breathed in, and so much negative thought and stresses have overwhelmed our minds that the body has lost its natural ability to heal. I am a victim, they claim of genetics because of my mother having glaucoma.

I must tell you that at present, I am not one to corrupt the body with unhealthy foods, alcohol, or drugs. I smoked cigarettes for many years as a broadcaster and student, but I stopped smoking when I came to America. So yes, I had my fair share of poisons.

And I would say it is the blunder of youth. Every one of us does something that is juvenile, and as my father said often, "Youth is a blunder." We all make mistakes.

On the other hand, I believe what you wrote that the body when allowed, when given the correct nutrition, will heal itself. The nutrition part is good, but not wholly expedient. It is possible to say that no matter how well a person eats, there's a time to die.

Now some may think this fatalist and suggest that I am running away from myself. That is practically impossible. My self is around and within me. If I run away from it, I die. I have known people who eat the best, fed themselves the best, did not smoke, did not drink alcohol and use other substances, and they died in traffic accidents. The CEO of Survey Monkey, a multimillionaire at 47, fell from his tread- mill and hit his head... dead. He ate well!

I have known cultures, particularly those in the east, where people live late into their nineties, strong and doing challenging things. I had a grand aunt who walked three miles to her garden till her late eighties.

I am learning now that there are regions of the brain that support healing. The challenge is, since we were not cultured to look within as children, the challenge is finding a way to tap into that tremendous healing energy within us all. That is the key.

The body can rise to healing from all diseases, but we need know how or, at the best, step out of the way and let it heal. And this healing transcends the brain, even the mind.

We could talk about this forever. I could tell you about what I am doing now toward that healing. We need time and a safe line that will not cost you anything. Just imagine we talking for about an hour? What about Skype? Dominica is on my mind. The longing is profound, but I cannot allow it to frustrate me. Honestly, I long to see Dominica again and you soon. Let's be faithful.

Have you put unsafe substances, food, etc., into your body? Or is there something I do not know that you wish to share with me? My fervent hope is that you nurture a solid relationship with that which is within you. I long to be with you, to at least show you a point of entrance if it still matters. All in all, I am well and pressing on. This is the year, and I am happy that you're here with me. Looking forward to seeing you. Much love.

April 11, 2016

Stein

Who can doubt hearing your reticence or just the shy, sometimes hidden tendency. It's always so much of a delight just hearing you, your voice, its enthusiasm or reservation, its outburst or its quieting, and of course, the work voice as opposed to the one enjoying the party. Whichever it is, it's great and reminds me of the very first time I heard you. I love the same even today. Much love.

April 11, 2016

Jolita

You just always know the right time to call. I desperately needed that laugh this morning.

Just seeing that number appear on the screen this morning, I didn't know how to respond. I was not in the best of places. It has been a dark long weekend, but thank you, really, thank you for that call. You have sent some sunshine my way, and I am grateful.

Have yourself a blessed day.

Love, J.

I thank God for a friend like you!

April 11, 2016

Stein

What made your weekend dark and long, my dear? When can you tell me? This is a deep statement.

April 11, 2016

Jolita

I believe the one I call the love of my life is having another affair. He won't admit to it, but all the signs are there, and people keep telling me about it. I got so mad at him that I asked him to move out yesterday, and he did. I miss him, but I am still so mad at him for not admitting it to me. I am just so confused right now.

April 12, 2016

Stein

What are you crying about? Think of it. The same one who once brought you pleasure now causes you pain. You hate the pain as most of us would, and the pleasure, when you reflect on it, makes you miss him. It's a narrow space in which to move to an emotional balance. I will write to you every day until you ask me to stop—if you can stop me. You need support, and not many people can be told how you hurt. In many instances, friends whom you once depended on and who let you in on his infidelity can be the ones who desert you. What can you do now? You can only cry.

Sometimes you wonder whether he hurts also. He does, but he can always find rescue in the embrace of another woman. She now feels happy to have him all to herself. This too shall pass or become joyful.

Let us not wish anyone bad endings. If he and she were to become true lovers and live with each other forever and you remained hating him for hurting you, you will be the one hurting more.

So being the practical woman you are, you now must think of a way to salvage your emotion, both that which you shared with him and that which you now expend on the loss.

My ideas are a bit unorthodox. Yesterday I asked you to pray for him. I can well hear you saying, "Stein, you're mad. Pray for him? He hurt me." This is precisely why you should give thanks for having met him. That may be the catalyst for his return.

Then of course, you need take care of your balance emotionally. When a woman hurts, she drowns her hurt in some activity. Many take to reading. You mentioned being confused. Maybe this is an excellent time to begin reading extensively. Strange. Let your thoughts roam into other dimensions. They return with solutions, and you finally fall asleep on those nights when you really miss him. Let's begin by finding solutions for your well-being. Who knows? You may send me a note tomorrow or even today telling me that he has decided to come back. Then you turn to setting rules of engagement.

These are my thoughts for today. Tomorrow may awaken another set, nothing, or a full-blown outburst. Take it easy. Don't hurt yourself with anger and outrage. It's only for a moment, and there are billions of men in the world. It's the mistake of youth to think that when you're in love, this is the person for you, and when you lose him, your world has ended. No, darling. Your life has just begun.

Much love.

April 12, 2016
Jolita

Thank you. You are just too sweet. In my little world, I have encountered very few heartbreaks but this one really hit home. I expect a man to cheat, but not even wanting to own up to it after all is said and done is heart breaking. Making excuses after you have somewhat been caught is foolish to me. All I have been asking for was an apology, a simple "I'm sorry." Everybody makes mistakes, but if when pointed out, you still refuse to admit it is a mistake and apologize, then you really are not ready.

I miss him, and I know he misses me too, but I'm not going to accept him back into my life and my home unless I am sure he is ready to humble himself and take up responsibility for his actions. If a man can't humble for little things, then he will never be humble. I need a man that knows how to be humble and humbles himself when the time calls for it.

My heart, as usual, is stubborn-even if my head says stay away, he is no good. The heart will always go back for more. As you said, "The same one who once brought you pleasure now causes you pain." I think love is about pain and sacrifices. There will be good times, but we should always expect the worst of times. I believe that we all somehow know it is coming. That is why in the vows, they say "for better or worse." I definitely don't want that part in my vows. My vows got to say "as long as he behaves!" If I have to see worst, I won't just say it is a mistake. Next time I will show a man what a mistake is and how it can become a habit. I am okay today. I just think I needed time to pause on the thinking and focus more on the loving. We will be good soon.

April 13, 2016

Stein

How are you today? Did you allow him back in? This makeup is gonna be grand! Ha-ha! Let me know...

April 13, 2016

Jolita

Hi, I'm good. We are talking, but I haven't given him the permission to move back in yet. It is too early. He got to suffer a lil more. Just in hopes that he thinks twice before he does it again.

April 13, 2016

Stein

Is there something about you that would cause him to want to cheat? Have you looked carefully at yourself to try to find out what it is about you that would push him away every now and then?

April 13, 2014

Jolita

Well, he said I don't spend enough time with him. But he is also stating that he is not cheating; the girl is just a very good friend to him.

April 13, 2016

Stein

So the time you don't give him, he finds with the other woman. Seems contradictory to me that he lives with you, and yet he claims you do not spend enough time with him. You need a commitment. He's not ready for one. His body is with you, but his mind is somewhere else. He and this girl are more than just friends. Ask him whether they've ever hugged or kissed, and he goes on the defensive. You are right. It's gonna need time, and you, you must be patient "investigating" this one. Do not punish him, however, because no relationship falls apart on account of one person. Somehow, you are responsible for this too. If I knew him, I'd ask that he sends you flowers. Much love.

April 14, 2016

Jolita

What is left to do? I think I will let him come back home this weekend and then monitor him from there, 'cause I keep hearing he is still seeing her, but I am not sure myself. I think I need to satisfy myself and prove to my heart that he is not the one for me. He is a liar, and he is very unfaithful. I need to test this to see.

April 14, 2016

Stein

Okay. Remember, sex is just one aspect of love.

April 18, 2016

Jolita

He is gone. He never loved me. It must have all been about the sex. Don't call, I honestly can't talk this morning.

We made up Friday night into Saturday morning, but he went back to her for the rest of the weekend. Haven't seen him since.

April 18, 2016

Stein

Are you still speechless? When can I speak with you? Or will you send a note.

Much love.

April 19, 2016

Jolita

I'm trying my best not to cry. Holding it all in. I guess I can say I speak now. Once I am not thinking, I am good. But it is hard after you have dedicated your life to someone to have them just crush you to pieces and not be willing to even say sorry.

We made plans for the future. I had hope, and now I am not sure where I stand. I know I can find another, but it is not about finding someone else. My heart wants him; we were good together, and my son loves him. We are almost a family. I am not willing to lose all that, but I am not going to push myself on him if that is not what he wants.

April 20, 2016

Jolita

I'm sitting at work and thinking about our conversation this morning. What is the greatest gift I can give myself? I believe the greatest gift of all is love, but we give that to our self every now and then.

We also find people who give us love, so I think it is enough for now.

The next thing that came to my mind is to give myself a better life. How do I go about doing that? Securing a future beyond this workplace and making the most of myself.

I have always just settled for what I have, and honestly it has not gotten me far but only to the place where I am and where I believe I need to be. My focus has been on my family and making a better life for my son, and of course, trying to find us a good husband and father. My son is about to start school now, and I am still trying to complete my house. I chose to build my house over going back to school and further my studies. I have a structure on pillars, but with the way things are turning now, I need to build the downstairs to put to rent, and then I can think of me.

School is getting more and more expensive, and I would prefer my son gets what he needs to succeed first. My time is almost done for studies. With my salary and my commitments, it is difficult to do anything else. I am trying to do what I can do now for him, and then I can think of myself.

I am not ready mentally nor financially to go back to school. Everybody is studying now, and there is no room for progress. It is a struggle, and the worst thing is that it doesn't matter how much education you have. It all depends on availability of space and who you have behind you. It's all about pulling the right strings, and right now all strings are occupied. Right now the best gift I can give myself is hope for a brighter future for my son.

Please note that I have not given up on me yet. I just need to be ready mentally and financially. I have been rethinking criminal justice—I am not sure that this is of much worth right now. I think I should go into business, marketing, finance, or something of that sort to enhance what I am doing here. Going back to my work now.

Much love, J.

April 21, 2016

Stein

Appreciate your honesty and candor. It is critical that you evaluate your own situation. You did just that.

In the long run, you've constructed a priority list, and from your perspective, this gift of education is not up on that list. Who knows, you are likely to find this emerging as your son goes through ranks of learning.

Does not matter to me whether you find reference educationally in criminal law, artificial intelligence, economics, business, finance, geography, or languages and human behavior. I sure hope that throughout our conversations, I did not suggest that this was something you had to do. In fact, I hope you do not feel pressured to meet those goals. This should flow naturally -- your education interest, that is.

I simply believe that beyond satisfying your need for family and meeting the needs of your son, you too can find self-actualization in a matter of interest transcending your everyday interests. As long as I'm around, I shall speak of that potential in you. Whether you turn to it is up to you. You should look to you at twenty-six to find ways of making you stronger. You have to get to thirty, thirty-five, forty, etc. What is the rush to bring back or find a man when you have barely been to you, a you with such huge potential?

You write, "I have always just settled for what I have, and honestly it has not gotten me far but only to the place where I am and where I believe I need to be." And where you believe you "need to be," is this settling for the mediocre, as you say for what you "have," which when negated suggests what you don't have? Where you believe you need to be has not done much for you either.

Forgive me if this is noncompromising. You're not in the best of moods. I need you to use this difficulty in your relationship to make a decision about where you can go from here without a man. A man will come. And after looking at all possibilities, if you find it impossible to do something wholesome for yourself without one, then take him back or find another.

Much love.

April 26, 2016

Stein

Ethiopians say, "When in doubt, stop to pick flowers." A woman was on a journey and found herself at the intersection of four roads. She became confused, not knowing which of the roads to take. She paused a while, and it occurred to her that instead of worrying, why not stop a while to eat something. She sat on the side of one of the roads and took to eating. While doing that, another traveler came along and pointed out the right way. Much love.

April 27, 2016

Jolita

I am picking flowers!

April 27, 2016

Stein

What an exciting lover you are!

April 28, 2016

Jolita

How can you say that? I only try to be. If you are not going to be excited about love, then why love?

April 28, 2016

Stein

Are you again going into love? Given your experiences, you're not likely to be excited. But you need remember that love comes before the excitement about love. You're hurting still, and because of this, I am hurting too. Remember that love comes before the excitement over love. You are excited about the love you give yourself. This agape is different from the erotic love you try to share. Agape is pure and unconditional.

You know what erotic love is. You also know what filial love is, but there is love that flows right through you. This is the source of all love.

But telling you this does not stop the confused state. What do you feel inside your belly when you sit still? Is this the love you want to possess? Love, I believe, is stirring in you, but you do not identify it as love. Love to you can be found in another's appreciation of you-a slightly displaced view when you're hurting. Time will heal, my dear. Just be patient. Don't know if I'll hear or read you tomorrow, so be careful who you share your emotions with. Remember, love stirs in you and loves you.

Much love,

Your friend

April 29, 2016

Jolita

I have a love, the best kind, and I have found it in you, a love to cherish, a love that never fades. Thank you.

It is a very busy day today, but I just had to say thank you, thank you for giving this rare love. You are like that last drop of water in the desert.

Thank you. You always know just what to say.

Love, J.

May 23, 2016

Stein

I have not been able to talk with you in a while. I do hope you are well. Is everything back to normal? Is he at home again?

I gather at some point in time you're going to say, surely, there's a time and a season for every purpose under heaven. There's a time to embrace and a time to refrain from embracing. There's a time to speak with and a time to be silent.

Despite these wise words, I still miss your notes, so full of fire and life. When will you write again?

Have you decided on your career path or profession? I find the words career and profession sometimes to be so loaded with hard work rather than "smart work" that I hesitate to use them. I may wish to ask instead, have you found an interest? Have you begun to cut that path? Think big, start small. Should there be a rush or a call to compliance with times set, goals set, etcetera? No. Just asking....... I will wait ten years if that's what it takes for you to find that which holds and is likely to hold your attention and passion for a lifetime!

Much love.

May 23, 2016

Jolita

My dear Stein, I am so sorry. I am all right. I am still struggling to move on, but I know I will get there. I just have to keep telling myself that, but I so just want to reverse time. It feels like I am losing my husband and friend. I don't want to lose him, but he is not good for me. I told him what I wanted, and all he is doing is pretending with me. It's hard to move on when you bring someone so deep into your life. He was my everything, and nothing I can do now will bring that back. It may slow down his progress if I bring him back home, but it won't stop him from seeing his other girlfriend. I just have to find a way to move on.

I am trying to write, but there is no more fire and life. The fire outed in the flood. Life is still on the balance, fighting to survive. I can't find anything to write about.

I have not found anything that drives my interest or drives me. I don't know what to choose, what path is pulling. I think it is because I am too caught up in my own world to figure it out. It just takes time, but things will happen, I believe that.

How are you doing? How is the progress coming along?

Love,

J.

May 23, 2016

Stein

Despite these wise words, I still miss your notes, so full of fire and life ... when will you write again?

I am trying to write but there is no more fire and life, the fire outed in the flood. Life is still on the balance, fighting to survive. I can't find anything to write about. I have not found anything that drives my interest or drives me. I don't know what to choose, what path is pulling.

Solution begins to emerge from the rush. I think it is because I am too caught up in my own world to figure it out. One possibility...

Here's another thought possibility. It just takes time, but things will happen.

This above is not just a passing thought. I am not being mean or callous when I say you are still strong. Dig deeper to find confidence and strength. It is all in you. I believe that.

The moments of confusion, sense of loss, and deep doubt can be depressing. But you see, it is out of this darkness that you emerge. In fact, you may not even have to emerge. It is in this darkness that a star emerges. You are...

You must be a very emotional woman, shouting when you're angry, telling anyone what's on your mind. Let go of all of this.

Think of it: you are only hurting yourself. Long before you were born, your heart was formed. A heart that is broken has to mend. As you state so correctly, give it time, give it time.

Hey, and remember, the fire never dies. It consumes. Let it purify you!

Life is in water. Grab water and you can never hold it. Go gently into it with your hands, and you feel it even while it feels you.

You are more than just a husband or boyfriend. Strength to overcome is in you. Use your energy to search you out, not in bringing him back. If he's destined to come back, he will. In the meantime, come back to you. You are overwhelming yourself with hurt, and that just grows exponentially.

Okay, be still.

June 2, 2016

Jolita

Good morning, my dear Stein,

How are you doing this lovely morning? It has truly been a while. Tell me about your healing process. How is it coming along?

How is the family, especially the little one, the joy of the bunch?

I do have a Facebook account; it is under my name.

Tell me, what has Stein been up to lately?

I want to say thank you for helping me in my dark moments. I was confused. Didn't know how to feel, how to think, or what to believe, and you helped me. Your inspirational talks kept me going and still have me pushing on. He wants to come back into my life, and honestly I am not busy and not even concerned about this. I just don't care what he does anymore. I realize to myself that I am stronger than that, and I don't need him or anybody in my life. I am a complete being. He is just an extra, and when this extra is messing up this being, you get rid of it 'cause it's not a necessity.

Thank you so much.

Have a blessed day. Hoping to hear from you soon.

Love, J.

June 2, 2016

Stein

There's nothing unusual out here. The world believes that Americans are confused trying to determine which of the two forces they will adopt as President. Let's see what the result will be. As far as I know, whoever enters the White House's Oval Office is changed from that time-all campaign promises and standpoints disappear as he or she confronts imperatives of those who rule America and by extension the financial world! Obama appeared to turn gray over that discovery of a letter left for him by Bush. Whoever comes after him will find a letter at that desk, the contents of which change their dreams and aspirations regarding this great nation.

In the midst of this raging state, I seek out my burgeoning self, its breath, its spirit. Its body's healing stumbles and rises-I surely believe changes in my life could move on faster. But up to August/ September, times and seasons are more than likely to be slower until the great thrust begins. So if you feel kind of slow and things seem not to be flowing favorably, hang in there; it won't be long. In the meantime, use the time to inform yourself.

There's nothing happening around you that is of greater significance than what can happen and is happening inside you, with you and you working with and engaging yourself in meaningful learning. All learning does not happen in school.

At present, I am using a protocol of alternative approaches. Since my eyes have been so accustomed to using medication from the pharmaceutical business, it is taking a bit of time to bounce back or align to this new protocol. Much of this new approach involves the use of algae-blue/green algae, green algae protein quite a few underwater products.

My eyes are raging, and my whole head wants to push out another eye, a new one, I imagine. It may all be imagination after all. Thing is, a fire burns in my soul that keeps me knowing that all will be well. Somehow, by some means, through some favorable appearance, product, dream. or vision, I am about to come upon a protocol that will rebuild damaged spots in my eyes.

Ophthalmologists do not think so; they say as long as a person is blind from glaucoma, that person is blind. But their own best universities are investing heavily in stem cell and blindness. Were they to use it diligently, they would restore the sight of every blind person under the sun because stem cells build back the entire damaged organ in any body.

In medical school, they teach students that the optic nerve, once damaged, cannot be restored. That's how far they got. Nerve tissue to them is still mystery. Too vast, too much like the Internet!

You may remember writing me, saying, "Not by might, not by power, but by your spirit." I think this spirit is energy, breath, law inscribed in my heart and mind. I'm really pushing and engaging this gift of energy which God has placed within me. In the final analysis, this is all I have remaining.

Now somebody may come along representing God's gift to my healing. Thus, even while we look into ourselves, we cannot be so introverted that we miss an expression of miraculous works: a wonderful, gifted, blessed person; another idea; another way of knowing, another ophthalmologist, indeed another beloved optometrist. Keep an open mind, a steadfast hand!

As for this love affair, I think I've been talking about this all along. Change has come to your life. You're wiser now. Give thanks for the change and the new life opened to you. Be accountable to no one but yourself and you'll see how magnificently you'll find what you need.

I'm not afraid for you at all. Just think you needed to know you. I will not even suggest anymore what I think you can and should do. You are quite able to take a decision at this point in your life.

Listen to your heart, study your thoughts, feel your emotions. Learn to laugh at yourself. Hum when you're sad. And at times, just let go and be still.

Listen to your breath or just sense your body heaving gently!

I am so happy to hear from you.

Much love.

July 6, 2016

Jolita

Hello, good morning.

I am looking for a friend. He goes by the name of Steinberg Henry, but I call him Stein. Have you seen him? Do you know him? Could you tell him I asked about him? He is a really nice guy if you get to know him. Very intelligent, bubbly personality and the best friend anyone could ever ask for.

How are you, my dear Stein? I know it has been a while.

But I am here, and I am great.

How is the family doing? Tell me about the little grands.

Most importantly, how is the healing going along?

I would love to hear from you. I miss you.

Have a great day.

Love, J.

July 6, 2016

Stein

Responded immediately in the hope of hearing your voice, and I did! No matter what I said and how

I said it, it is always out of great pleasure and delight that I speak with you. Just hearing you is enough.

I sure hope you are really great because I would hate to know that you're still hurting yet telling me you're great. This matter has to be resolved once for all on whichever lines the boundaries fall.

Since fasting began thirty days ago, my eyes have crossed the most dangerous places. I have moved from seeing some to seeing nothing, fog and darkness. But always, a fire burns in me. I am confident that I shall find a good report and have my fortunes, including my eyes, restored to brightness.

I go to the patio after dropping the liquid into my eyes, find the warm rays of sunlight rising straight, and ask the light of the sun to penetrate my eyes deep into my optic nerve. I thank God for the light of the sun. It may seem unorthodox, but this is the path I've chosen. Sometimes I feel frustration rise in me, and I breathe it, telling myself and thoughts that we've come too far now to be tired and frustrated. Sometimes I weep in prayer.

Thing is, there is more to sight loss than biology and genetics, disease, and other explanations. J., the vista beyond seeing eyes is vast, glorious, full of splendor, majestic, holy, and strikes fear. A beautiful blessing about this inner vision is that it does not kill. It loves!

As for my grandson, he's almost eighteen months. He's walking, running, screaming, choosing, responding, shaking his head no, rolling on the floor when he's not pleased, dancing, eating well, and growing long. His mother and grandmother are well-pleased!

Just came out of thirty days of fasting... another matter. Seemed like this exercise opened my eyes. Could see your hair and... Only Homeland Security heard. How's the new male interest, or are you taking a sabbatical? Well, whoever it is, tell him you have an older guy who loves you in a special way, not to 'cause you hurt. Careful, Stein!

Good hearing you, my dear.

Much love.

July 8, 2016

Jolita

Hello, my dear Stein,

It was really nice hearing from you again. You always have a way of bringing me back to a place of complete happiness. I am still hurting, but I am not letting this hurt get the better of me. I think very little on it, and I can say that I believe I am moving on. I am smiling, laughing, and maybe even flirting a little. It has been a long journey, but I can finally see the end. No new boyfriends yet, just friends. I need to find my happiness in me first.

It is great that you are fasting, but now it has set you behind on your progress to rejuvenating sight. You are strong, so I know that this was only a minor setback, but it is for the best. The body is evolving. It is going beyond the ordinary. It is pushing and fighting, and that is all you! Continue what you are doing. You may get frustrated but don't ever give up. You have seen some difference since you have started so push onward. It's a fighting battle, but God is good. He has granted you sight to do so many things in the past, , and then he transformed that sight into some- thing deeper; now you see things on a deeper level. By the grace of God, you will one day be able to see things on both levels. Remember in his words. He said he will never give us more than we can handle, so just trust in him and know that all will be okay. I am so glad to hear that your grandson is progressing nicely. Hope he continues like this and becomes as curious as my son is.

Have yourself a blessed day today.

Love, J.

July 8, 2016

Stein

I read your letter, and immediately this verse from a poem titled "The Road Not Taken," by Robert Frost came to mind:

> I shall be telling this with a sigh
> Somewhere ages and ages hence:
>
> Two roads diverged in a wood, and I—
>
> I took the one less traveled by,
>
> And that has made all the difference.

Love to you, wonder-filled woman. It is a delightful pleasure knowing you. Much love.

An extract from our past communication was selected and sent to Jolita. She was amazed by what she herself had written.

July 20, 2016

Stein

When you write, it's hard to believe I was part of those conversations. You're expressing a true advanced linguistic code. Do not dismiss them. In fact, they are so powerful that together we may decide to edit them for publication. I've thought about this long. There's so much reflection in your words, so rich a foray into the philosophical and spiritual, I cannot resist seeing their potential. Of course, the context would have to be explained/described, and any suggestion that we needed each other with a passion may well be edited out (LOL). Tell me what you think.

July 20, 2016

Jolita

I think it's a good idea. I believe they are very powerful. There is a lot of substance in those passages, so much life encouragement and emotions. It's not just words. When we speak together, it gets deep. It is like a new discovery into life, a different way of looking at things, an eye-opener.

September 14, 2016

Stein

Good day to you beloved. Found the excerpt below a note exchange between us and, your response just blows my mind! My December 9, 2015, mail read,

> Thought of you today. Even attempted to call you, touch base with your effervescence and smile. I sensed today was full, and you, knowing you apply yourself to the work at hand, would be busy multitasking.
>
> This text is slipping into touching. It needs to stay at the level of criminal law. Remember that initial, that original oeuvre.
>
> Must find you a song for inclusion in my next mail today.
>
> I read Derek Walcott's writing in the poem "Parang"-"flesh upon flesh"

was the tune since the first cloud raise up to disclose the breast of the naked moon."

I breathed in to learn this inherent mystery.

Love to you.

Your December 9 response was,

Good morning,

You read very interesting poems. That simple line excited my morning a bit too much this morning. I kept rereading this line, putting myself in the position, trying to feel the intensity of this situation, fantasizing on the passion and fire between these two flesh. Oh gosh, the hunger, the yearning! This seems too intense, too emotional. The criminality in this situation is at a high. I do believe for this case to be properly judged, it needs to be evaluated at a different angle. I believe the situation needs to be relived and properly examined. The nature of this case calls for such things. Reading this case entices a lust that needs to go further than just in the mind of the listener, it needs to be felt.

I am going to leave it at that and return to work! It's always a pleasure hearing from you. Have a good day.

Love,

—J.

September 14, 2016

Jolita

Good morning,

This is a very interesting conversation. You read too many interesting conversations. Are you sure that was our conversation? Where were we? Oh my gosh.

September 14, 2016

Stein

Lemme tell you something, Miss. If you do not wish to be associated with your own text. let me know (LOL). I intend to send you just under eighty pages written between us over a twenty-month period.

You seemed surprised that you could have written such insightful literature. Is this the lure technique? Have you changed so dramatically having found someone new that you can no longer relate to a self that existed once upon a time?

I thought you had agreed for us to reread these texts, that you had set up the Skype for our review, and we were going to be creative in our editing, given the private nature of any such communication. I await your instructions. At the same time, just reading you is wonder-filled. Hey, are we going to do this edition?

Much love.

September 14, 2016

Jolita

Oh, oh, what did I do?

I believe that I lost myself, the me that you know and love. There is no new love, and maybe that is the problem. The lack of that particular type of love (eros) in my life has got me lost in memories. The me that we both love is stuck in between memories of a love that once was. It's sad. I am still looking for that young lady and hoping that she is still alive. She was always happy and full of life.

I did create the Skype account, but I am yet to actually start using it with you. That's my fault. I think I spend too much time at work and very little time with myself that when I get home, all I want to do is sleep. I'm sorry.

Love, J.

September 15, 2016

Stein

Didn't realize you were still hurting. I'm sorry if in any way, I seemed to rush you into a state of calm. Just as you are your fullness, in the final analysis, you will be.

The fact that you live on memory alone these days is in and of itself, not a bad exercise. Treat it, think of it as one of the moods, feelings which had to come to you. But it itself is not with you for no reason. You can no longer continue to be lost- -it may be rough, but you are being asked to find yourself, your "her" in the milieu. As you said this morning, the word just came. Thing is, you live in a beautiful mind. You compliment me for being this way on many occasions. As it is popularly said, it takes one to know one.

I care about your emotional being. In this regard, I am hoping that the self you speak about as being apart from you sitting now or standing, with height, weight, bone structure, dressed in corporate blue, pleasant, and, of course, full of life and joy is real. And when the self is real, it experiences a range of emotions. Sadness is one of them, but even it too (sadness, that is) agrees that it carries windows that open into spaces and places of reflection. Tell you, in the final analysis, you will be a much stronger woman. But do not allow this past experience to make you bitter, hateful of men, or cynical. That is the enemy's wish. You need read differences between a road that disciplines and one that is wicked. Indeed, God's children rise above all.

Love you.

September 19, 2016

Jolita

Good morning,

I may still be healing, but I'm okay. I still have thoughts of what was and could be, but I am confident that I made the right choice for me. I'm looking back, but I'm not going back to it.

As a songwriter says, "It is better to have loved and lost than never to have loved at all." It was great while it lasted, but it wasn't great enough to last.

The me that I am seeking is found in my happiness and stuck there. In complete happiness and self-satisfaction, I can find the me that I need, but the road to get there is so long and rough, it is taking me forever, or maybe I am not trying hard enough.

You said to me, "All that you need is inside of you." What then are you looking for? What is it that you seek? All the sight that you need in side of you—you see better than anyone that I know. Your sight is deep; you see into a person. You are just perfect. Regaining your other sight may change the way you see things. It may cause you to rely more on what you can see and less on the true person at hand. I am not trying to discourage you. I just want you to know that you are perfect the way you are and that you have achieved much without your sight and will continue to strive to achieve more.

Have a blessed day. Love, J.

September 19, 2016

Stein

Beloved,

The line you quoted, "Better to have loved and lost," comes from a poem written by Alfred Lord Tennyson. The poem was titled "In Memoriam AHH." Somebody thought it wise to place these lines in a song. Observe that the poem is long and your selected line is at verse 27. It's beautiful. Why do I have within me the deepest feeling that you'll love again?

> XXVII
>
> I envy not in any moods
>
> The captive void of noble rage, The linnet born within the cage, That never knew the summer woods: I envy not the beast that takes His license in the field of time, Unfetter'd by the sense of crime, To whom a conscience never wakes; Nor, what may count itself as blest, The heart that never plighted troth But stagnates in the weeds of sloth; Nor any want-begotten rest.
>
> I hold it true, whate'er befall;

I feel it, when I sorrow most;

'Tis better to have loved and lost Than never to have loved at all.

September 19, 2016

Stein

Beloved,

"The road is long," the songwriter sang, "with many a winding turn that leads us to who knows where / who knows where / but I'm strong / strong enough to carry 'her' / she ain't heavy / she's my sister." In the original, they sing, "he's my brother."

It is not a container metaphor being used when I say all that is needed is inside you. There is a stillness in us which calms the anxiety of these times. I am aware that you want immediate results, and so your patience thins. It is rough, but maybe not rougher than any other road.

Every man and woman you see anywhere in this world is carrying a matter of concern inside. Look at yours not in comparison to others, but for what it is.

I gather you think of lungs, heart, intestines, liver, etcetera, when you think inside, but there's breath as well. I do not want to bore you with the same story regarding meditation. That story that happened long ago when you were in love and the possibility of searching for that space was real.

You are emotional. Most of that energy cannot be spent doing monotonous work. God speaks to us through monotony and even more through diversity of occupations. Set aside a bit of time for you alone beloved.

You are working. You are walking. You are talking. You can dress, determine your colors. You eat, drink, laugh. You are alive. Though your heart is heavy, you can carry it, and when your heart is light, you will remember when it was heavy every now and then. Gosh, I wish we could talk!

-Steinbergdasilva

September 21, 2016

Jolita

Happy birthday!

A happy, happy birthday to you, my dear Stein. I do hope you make the best of it. Do something different. Do something out of the ordinary. Do something you are going to remember. Have a blessed day.

Love, J.

September 22, 2016

Jolita

Hello, hello. How was the birthday? I hope you didn't spend it like you spent all your other days? How are you feeling? Do you feel younger, more energized, spirit-filled? Love, J.

September 22, 2016

Stein

No. I feel like an ancient man who has just emerged from a formation of stars. I feel like an old, old, old man who has just burst forth from the trunk of a tree.

I feel like a woman who has just given birth and beholds, looks upon her newborn with joy, pleasure, and delight. I feel like a newborn star, a newborn tree, a newborn child. I am in a "wonderspace," a spacious place with a delightful inheritance.

I feel like Jolita, who asks and asks, and the universe looks into my eyes and says, "It is your time." And I ask is it the same for my beloved Jolita, and the answer came.

I was asked to hold the answer for a brief time, about seven days, until she had cleared one hurdle. There's a matter she still struggles with. This she should cross over within the next few days.

I said, "I love Jolita and would like you, Great Spirit, Wonderful Counselor, to counsel her. Guide and enrich her life with true and everlasting love." And since I requested this everlasting, true love for you, I received the same. How awesome? How excellent! I will tell you this—the party is this weekend.

Love,

Steinbergdasilva

September 22, 2016

Jolita

Wow that must have been a birthday. Well, I am sure you will enjoy the party. Save a dance for me.

September 23, 2016

Stein

So what is your Skype name/address?

September 27, 2016

Jolita

Morning,

I am not good at technology. I believe I have more than one Skype accounts, but the one I am signed in on today says

I see you had a great birthday party. I saw a picture with you at the party. You look great, handsome, and you have a beautiful family. That was a beautiful family picture. Wish you a blessed day today.

Love, J.

October 18, 2016

Stein

Does this year-end mark the end of our communication?

I think of you.

I hope you're well and as promised, taking care of yourself. Love.

December 1, 2016

Jolita

Good day,

How is my dear Stein doing today? How is the healing process coming along?

I just thought I would drop an email to let you know I still care. I know I have been distant and we have not talked in a long while, but I am still here, and I have not abandoned you. I am still your friend.

Right now I am trying to get more involved in church activities, motivating and encouraging the younger children in the things of God, trying to put a spark in their hearts to want to do things in the Kingdom of God and to be more spiritually grounded. Too many of our young children have moved away from the things of God, from church, from a decent way of living and have found themselves engulfed with the evils of this world. It is ridiculous, the simple things that people lose their lives for. I believe that with a little love and a little spiritual enlightenment, the young people can find themselves on a better path in life. They can find something to do with their time instead of wasting it looking for trouble and they will better be able to make reasonable, problem-solving decisions.

Well, for now I am going to get back to work. Will talk to you sometime soon. Please tell me a little about what is currently going on in your life's journey. Once again, thank you for being the friend that you are.

Have a blessed day.

Love, J.

December 12, 2016

Stein

After eleven days of receiving your letter, I am sending you this update. It is a living hope that we roommate with, and I thank God for the friend.

The healing process? The actual physical eyes have not improved significantly over the months. I am at a crossroad regarding what should be my next experiment/decision. This gives me time to rest a bit, find more sleep, and embrace longer meditation times being suggested to me by God's Great Spirit.

As for medication, you know that I do not indulge, and as for plants, herbs, supplements, etc., I have even become skeptical of these since they are generally suffused with other substances, fertilizers to enhance potency and growth.

I am not a purist, but we have come to know certain things. So what is the next move? Energy from within, tapping on the Spirit, moving the breath, reflecting on the things I have known over the years to guide, and this statement running through my entire being: everything you need is inside you!

I am moved by the promise that the same power that brought Jesus Christ from the dead lives in me.

On this path, the physical is not delivering up results yet, but it will come along clearly in its own time. I am hopeful and joyful! I am joyful too that at this tender age, you have decided to share with the younger ones the ways and Word of God. Girl, they're learning to use dance to praise God. How magnificent. There's so much we could share if only we could speak using Skype. I am not yet mobile, since I work from home. I have seen WhatsApp for PC, but I have not taken time to set that up...

Over the last three months, I have been doing computer training designed to add to the formal knowledge received both before Microsoft (as a graduate), and post-the-mouse into early use of screen readers. It's powerful stuff.

Been engaged, and since you are too, I gather we're using our time wisely. I am still of the view that people act in tandem, and distance does not separate spirits. I pray that the Holy Spirit, which speaks to us all truths, continue to guide your work and move the laws of God put in your mind and written on your heart.

I miss you deeply, but I can live with that.

—Steinbergdasilva

December 12, 2016

Stein

And when you find time, YouTube "divine dance institute."

—Steinbergdasilva

The next response would be long in coming, and I think it was stirred by a telephone call made by Jolita.

March 21 2017

Jolita

I enjoyed our conversation last night, as usual rich in content and enriching in thought. I am so thankful to have a friend like you.

The mind is a composition of thoughts, I learnt last night, so I am trying to release some of these thoughts and actually see them flow freely.

I want to thank you for finding your way into my life. God works in strange ways. All it took was one business conversation, and I had a friend for life. The impact you made on my life is one that has somehow shaped me into the person that I am today, mentally and spiritually. My journey with you has been one filled with laughter and joy, growth, humility, and so much more. You help me look at things from a different angle.

There is so much that I want in life, so much that I want to accomplish, and I have come to the realization that I have accomplished so much already, and I have done much more than I actually recognize. I thank God for it all as I push forward to accomplishing more.

Thank you, Stein, for the impact you made on my life. You have opened windows in my heart that I never knew were there. You have gravitated yourself to my present being and have touched me in places even I didn't feel. Your words are words of life. The very sound of your voice awakens something in me that keeps me motivated, keeps me moving. Your physical eyesight is weakened, but your spiritual one is strengthened. I can assure you that this was not only for your benefit but for mine also. Your words have become deep. There is strength in what you write and say. You bring life to words. Never thought I would meet someone as filled as you. This verse comes to me as I think of you. They are drawn from Proverbs 27:17: "Iron sharpeneth iron; so a man sharpeneth the countenance of his friend."

You sharpen me, the friend I have never met face-to-face. Despite the distance, you have always been there for me. You have been my rock in troubled times. God has used you in so many ways to reach out to me. Thank you for allowing God to use you, my friend, and thank you for being you to me. You are always in my prayers. Love, J.

March 22, 2017

Stein

It is a wonderful thing—this Spirit of the living God deposited in us. Thank you for being so gracious. Thank you for being you. Your power of expression has gained tremendous strength from our first note in March 2015. Yes, it is that recent. I remember once the longing was like that of a baby for its mother's milk. Then there was the time for everything, and we followed that law. I do not know whether you will write again or whether I will write again, but this does not matter now. What matters now is that I'm responding to you.

I need another conversation like the one we had Monday night. You know I got the feeling that that conversation could've gone on into wee hours of the morning, and we would still be awake listening. And then, we reached a mutual silence and laughter at the end.

It has been good knowing you. It is a strange find given that it was merely a business call that brought us together. As a consequence, we have been able to amass these words, this collection of emotions in narrative form which still stuns me reading them two years later. It didn't seem that anything or any- one else existed.

Though I missed you, when you wrote to tell me what you were doing in the church, I first hoped that you were not so grieved that you just went to that house of consolation. Then I thought that this might just be one of your talents being developed. Liturgical dance. How magnificent! I hoped that you would return to writing because there was so much that I could share with you to deepen your practice. It also occurred to me that you had and would have a lot to say as you forayed into these new praise practices. God is wonderful. The Holy Spirit tells us all truth! I am so delighted that you're passing that way. As you stated, iron sharpens iron, and indeed, our total conversations and collection of exchanges have surely sharpened our understanding of our individual selves and of each other. I am happy we found each other. Put another way, I am delighted that we were made to meet, share, and exchange. Thanks for your presence, your encouragement and support. Whenever mention is made of my eyes in your letters, what you write is always so positive and purpose-filled.

Thanks for keeping that clarity of vision regarding my sight and search for cure and healing. The journey has been long and continues. But you know what's great? Each day, something is revealed to me in the Spirit, to my mind and in my body. I enjoy the fact, yes, the fact that the Spirit of the Living God moves in me. It is more correct to say, I move in the Spirit of the Living God. Just imagine, you are called to write these sayings you've written to me! How glorious! How honored I am! As stated earlier, I found Hebrews 8 and Jeremiah 31 to carry that message about the new covenant and the putting of laws in our minds and their writing on our hearts. You're well on your way to becoming that fullness in woman. I am joyful to have the opportunity to be there, to be with you and to share words and breaths with you.

Love, S.

April 25, 2017

Jolita

How are you doing? I know I have somehow abandoned you. It has been a few rough weeks; my grandfather got a slight stroke, and it has been hectic for my family. My mom and I are the only two who are really there with him, and we were told to give him twenty-four seven surveillance. The body is getting stronger, but in a case like his and at his age, we are told to be on guard. I had to abandon the comfort of my home and bed to stay with him for two weeks. I just returned to work today. He has moved in with me, so I still have some adjusting to do.

All isn't bad with me. I have found a new love. Not replacing you at all but replacing what I once had. You can never be replaced for you have a special place in my heart. I have been helping a friend go through some difficult times in his life, and during this time, we seem to be getting closer, both afraid to find ourselves at the place where we once were but willing to give us a fair chance to love. It is not concrete, for his problems are just climaxing, but we are going to get through them and make each other happy. That is the plan. I take this to God and hope that this path is the right path for me at present.

How is Stein? How is the eyesight coming along? I miss you. I think I need to make an afternoon to talk. It is becoming way too long again. How is the family doing? Tell me about the young one. I need to know where Stein is and what he is up to at present. Love, J.

July 20, 2017

Stein

This is the only man who could ever love you. Ha-ha. He is programmed to come into your life in times of need and celebration. I attach for your wonder, a note from you to me sent March 21, 2017. Recently.

Whenever you wrote, your words said much to you as they did and do to me today. You are wonder-full. I do not say these because of pleasure we found in each other's bodies. No. I have higher forms of evidence (evidence being so common in usage these days of political intrigue).

I have beautiful evidence from the thousands of words you wrote to me. You can only be charged and tried in the court of love. You too shall be made free in the court of love. Bless you. Now read your healing words:

> I enjoyed our conversation last night. As usual, rich in content and enriching in thought. I am so thankful to have a friend like you. The mind is a composition of thoughts-I learnt last night—so I am trying to release some of these thoughts and actually see them flow freely.
>
> I want to thank you for finding your way into my life. God works in strange ways. All it took was one business conversation and I had a friend for life. The impact you made on my life is one that has somehow shaped me into the person that I am today, mentally and spiritually. My journey with you has been one filled of laughter and joy, growth, humility and, so much more. You helped me look at things from a different angle.
>
> There is so much that I want in life, so much that I want to accomplish, and I have come to the realization that I have

accomplished so much already, and I have done much more than I actually recognize. I thank God for it all as I push forward to accomplishing more.

Thank you, Stein, for the impact you made on my life. You have opened windows in my heart that I never knew were there. You have gravitated yourself to my present being and have touched me in places even I didn't feel. Your words are words of life. The very sound of your voice awakens something in me that keeps me motivated, keeps me moving. Your physical eyesight is weakened, but your spiritual one is strengthened. I can assure you that this was not only for your benefit but for mine also. Your words have become deep. There is strength in what you write and say. You bring life to words. Never thought I would meet someone as filled as you. This verse comes to me as I think of you. They are drawn from Proverbs 27:17: "Iron sharpeneth iron; so a man sharpeneth the countenance of his friend."

You sharpen me, the friend I have never met face-to-face. Despite the distance, you have always been there for me. You have been my rock in troubled times. God has used you in so many ways to reach out to me. Thank you for allowing God to use you, my friend, and thank you for being you to me. You are always in my prayers. Love, J.

July 21, 2017

Jolita

Good day, my Stein.

Greetings to you from an older woman, a friend of the past, in the present, and for the future. How are you, my friend? It has been ages. I haven't written like this to you. I feel this side of me quickly dying, crumbling to pieces, disappearing with time. There seems to be no time left. Is it that time is moving faster now than before, or is it that we have so much more to do that we lost track of time in itself? I miss you, Stein. No matter the distance, you have always been the one pushing and cheering me on. A friend that sticketh closer than a brother-that's who you are; determined to light the sparks and warm hearts that may come your way. Thank you for being such a friend to me. I love you for that. Even when we don't speak, you are forever in my prayers and in my heart.

Tell me about you. I have missed so much these couple months. Tell me about your sight's progress and about your grandkids. It has been a while.

My birthday was okay. I got older. Not sure about that wiser part but older for sure. I recently lost my grandmother, so instead of being in a celebration, I'm a bit depressed. I rejoice for there is no more suffering, but I mourn for the lack of her presence with us. It's nature taking its course, making way for another generation. I had an addition to the family the same day she passed away. She received one more granddaughter. It is a birthday to remember.

Please take care of Stein for me. I love him so much, and I await the day that we get to meet face-to-face. Much love, J.

Between July 22, 2017, and January 7, 2018, I heard nothing from Jolita. I missed her. Jolita had found new relations, and those had to be nurtured. I had myself embarked on a training program using screen-reading technology. That was intense. On many occasions, I felt disappointed, but Jolita needed time to focus on this fresh love affair. And we all know how exciting new love can be. I think I became keenly aware that if I respected my friend, I had to step back and allow her to nurture that relationship which had just blossomed in her life. Jolita and I might've communicated in the month of August, but our exchanges had become so sparse that after a while, we went our separate ways, never forgetting each other but facing the reality of our specificity. Things would become worse.

On September 18, 2017, two months after her July 21st letter, Dominica was hit by Hurricane Maria. The island was devastated. In one article appearing in Relief Web and titled "Dominica: The impact of Hurricane Maria-Disaster Profile" and posted January 31, 2018, the following appeared:

> *Hurricane Maria made landfall*
>
> *on the southwest coast of Dominica at 9:35pm on 18 September as a Category 5 hurricane, with 160 mph wind speed and higher gusts. The hurricane force resulted in intense storm surges, tor- rential downpour, overflowing raging rivers, and extremely high winds across the island which left 31 people dead, and 37 missing. 65,000 people, around 80% of the population, were directly affected and more than 90% of roofs were damaged or destroyed.*

Telecoms too were disrupted, impacting email and telephony. Jolita's community was affected, maybe even her house compromised. Clearly, it would be a while before I heard from Jolita, and when she surfaced, I was delighted.

January 8, 2018

Jolita

Good morning,

I am swamped at work. Sad to say, I hardly have the time to think of my next move. I know that this is wrong, but I can't help it at times, and then other times I really don't want to think of the next move. So many plans, so little time. I guess this is why it is said that the simplicity of life is far more rewarding than the treasures of this world. We do need a long Skype conversation, but for now the internet here is not good; I get missed calls, but I can't get a call or put in a call—the internet data drops. Messages go through, but it takes time. We really need to talk; I need to hear your voice, the voice that just rejuvenates and motivates me. I am otherwise doing good.

Enough about me, how are you doing? How is the family? I see you are still keeping up with the meditation. That is good. How are the eyes coping? Live simple, be happy, meditate on the things in life that matter, like family and love. You are an amazing man. You have lived an extraordinary life. You have experienced the beauty of life and have captured most of that in writing. Your life is a book worth reading, and I am grateful to find a friend like you. I hope that I can at least enjoy the thrill of meditation one day- -the peace it gives to you and the relaxation of mind is one to be envied.

I have never once forgotten about you. Have yourself a blessed day. Hoping to hear from you soon. Love, J.

January 9, 2018

Stein

It is not that I want you to respond to my call and stay on the line. I just need to know once how you are and how you're coping. As long as I know you are able to cope, this is okay. We do not have to rush to talk. We will when it becomes possible. The wrong that you speak about is circumstantial.

My meditation continues. I do not think it will ever stop, and yah, I know you look forward to that meditation. What I need to tell you in detail about my eyes and the methods I'm trying is not for the email. I'd prefer to speak with you. My sight is clearing, and the clearing is better today and then it goes to extremely blurred another day. The healing goes to the depth of the disorder and draws it out. This is when the fog or darkness occurs. Then suddenly, without my intervention or expectation, I see clearly. I feel so overjoyed when this happens. And it is not so much because I see for a few seconds-though this is absolutely wonderful—but it is because I am overwhelmed by the work of God in my life.

Make best use of your time. Whatever your station, give thanks. You have so much ahead of you. Everything we talked about and everything you dreamed of will begin to come to pass. You will then realize that building a foundation is real and necessary. But there is a sort of transition from foundation to implementation or beginning of activity.

I believe and think you are beginning to meet yourself, and that self is aligned with God's purpose in your life. Observe your life. Observe your life, its patterns, its repetitions, the events unfolding.

And then you may ask with so much to do, who has time to observe his/her own life? So many things unfold in any one day. The Holy Spirit intervenes for me with groanings that cannot be expressed.

-Your man

April 11, 2018

Jolita

Good morning and good day to you, my dear Stein, How are you doing this lovely day? How is your eyesight? I am sitting at work just done with a client and thinking how long it has been since I wrote to you. Time seems to be drifting away quickly, but never fear: it cannot drift me away from you. The days may be shorter, the nights may never seem to have appeared, but our friendship will always be speared.

So talk to me, Stein. Tell me what have you been up to for the past months? How is the family, especially the grandson?

Hoping to hear from you soon.

Love, J.

I thank God every time I think of you.

April 11, 2018

Stein

I thought about you throughout the day yesterday. You know, in the way you come to my mind, say hi, and flash out. It is better than nothing. I have missed you, but maybe we know others better from a distance. Nothing changes our friendship, and I thank God every time I think of you. It is still that real for me! You are still very fresh, radiant, and pure in and to my psyche. I pray that life remains kind to you and am assured that you continue to prosper abundantly and wisely.

I've completed writing *Calypso Drift and Water*. It is another long book, but I suggest that it may well be the last full-length one in the Calypso Drift series. Its subtitle is a bit surreal. It reads, *Reflective Eco Logic Moving Lyrical Imaginative Awareness*.

The other one or two in the Calypso Drift series, particularly the 2017 collection, will be written in collaboration with another writer. It will be shorter and more visual (LOL)! The first two go inward.

Then of course, I've edited Jolita, which is my next work. It is different from anything I've participated in. It is, too, controversial, but so passionate, so compassionate and caring, with spurts of sensuality! I love it. It should be about 180 pages long.

I will send the text to you for your reading. Please let me know which address I should send it to. And when you receive it, read on. Do not delay. Just press on with the reading so that we can complete it soon. After the exchange of letters, I thought of a section referred to as Two Epilogues. It is an opportunity for us two to respond to a matter that we each felt was not dealt with in the many correspondences. It is too the opportunity to reflect on what we had done, when it started, and our impressions on what it had become. Your epilogue should carry a bit of detail in its reflection. Essentially, take your time to write it to your satisfaction (i.e., after having read what we were able to assemble between us).

I am also compiling and editing a set of stories, poems, and other matters which I started in New York and extended into my stay here in Georgia. Quite fascinating to my psyche. As for my grandson here in Georgia, he's great, talking, critical with amazing powers of observation. I just love him. Remember too that up till now, I have six grands: five boys and one girl. Well, I look forward to seeing her soon. Can't wait. Heard she's quite intelligent and loving. Must be her parents…

I want you to write me back. I want to talk with you, but I suspect you do not have the time and the space. Another boyfriend has come again, and you need to take care of this one, not allowing any matter to disrupt you.

Let's hope the telecoms comes back on stream so that we can have a night talk from your community. As for my eyes, this requires another email.

Otherwise, I am well and busy.

Love, Stein

May 11, 2018

Jolita

Good afternoon,

I have been so caught up with work and, yes, my not-so-new associate that it is becoming difficult for me to even rest to think. I do want to apologize for that and my late response.

I did enjoy our days of conscious relaxed thoughts where you brought out in me deep thoughts that I never knew existed within what seemed like the tiny walls of my mind. For that I am forever grateful.

Do send me the documents, and as I read, I am sure that something beautiful will come to mind, bringing back and reminding me of the "us" that was and will forever be—a friend of thought and friends through thoughts. Never once met, we exist through the pages of this beautiful piece we have written. We were connected through our voices, then one letter after the next. Truly this is a friendship that needs not be put to rest.

I have finally gotten lights in my home this week. What a blessing, and surely enough I will get proper internet here soon. Eight months and counting since this disaster—God has been good.

How about you? What has been going on lately? How are those eyes? Are you finally able to recognize me as me? God's blessing upon you, my dear friend. I hope you have a wonderful night.

Love, J

Two Epilogues

This passage, drawn from Jolita's January 20, 2017 communication, has held my attention. It is a matter I do not have answers for. I can encourage her, but I myself do not even know my future and what it will bring.

Jolita wrote:

> I was just thinking about life, how things work out so strange. You never thought you would be here today. I am just wondering in the next twenty years, where will I be? Who will I be? How will I be? Will I still be here? The future is changing. No matter how we try, we can't stop what is to happen. It is said that we shape our own futures, we choose our own paths, but I don't believe that it is all up to us. We try our best, but if it is not part of God's plan, then no matter what steps we take to bring us where we want to be, it will not work. Barriers and limitations—that is a sign. Some we can overcome. Others are just there to direct us to the path we need to be on. Your barriers directed you to places and things you never expected, and every time a door of opportunity would close on you, a

> better door opens. When your sight started to give up, I know that frightened you. What would you do? How would you go on if you couldn't see? But here you are able to read what I am writing and communicating with me so well.

I was moved into a place I did not know. Not that I needed to answer or even to show that I knew the answer to this profound matter. I did not. I did not know where I would be tomorrow or in the next five minutes. As you said Beloved, the future is changing. No matter how we try, we can't stop what is to happen.

I went back to my favorite book to find Psalm 139 where, from verses 13–16, it is written:

> For You formed my innermost parts; you knit me [together] in my mother's womb. I will give thanks and praise to You, for I am fearfully and wonderfully made; wonderful are Your works, and my soul knows it very well. My frame was not hidden from You, when I was being formed in secret, and intricately and skillfully formed [as if embroidered with many colors] in the depths of the earth. Your eyes have seen my unformed substance; and in Your book

> were all written The days that were appointed for me, when as yet there was not one of them [even taking shape]

Unformed substance. If only we could know now what were essentials in that substance! In that substance were days appointed for you, your purpose, and its course. How many come to know this? It is formidable discipline to stand in your now, to stand in your own fire. In the final act of its consuming nature, we will be purified. For many, however, the trouble remains food, clothing, shelter, health, and education for themselves and their children, a friend or two. It is still that desire to feel good, to feel well, to feel joyful while that original utterance emerging from substance through formation in the womb to now does not speak its origin in known languages. Were that it would speak to all with clarity, nonambiguous without vacillation. And maybe it does, but few care to hear, much less to listen. Where you will be in the next twenty years may not be significant, but it shouts reality. If only you could know. What would you do then? You would begin to have confidence. You would need to take step by step. Friday will not become Wednesday of the next week because you rush to know what you see and know. Time as we know it will still move at the pace of the moon, save if you could quantum leap into that time. What if you could change the bad you foresaw, eradicate all obstacles, provide large sums of money for yourself and your family, eliminate all traces of sickness or disease, all failures, all losses. What if you could, as a consequence, remove all disasters, stop the flood and the rains, the wind and earth tremors. Where will I be in the next twenty years? Well, for one, you will be just under fifty years, and I will be just past eighty. I may be alive or dead, blind or seeing. You too may be dead or alive. Are these the options we have: dead or alive, blind or seeing? Let us wish and think otherwise. What happens when we begin to wish, like Christmas wishes, all good things for the ones we love? Are they likely to come to pass? Does what you or I speak matter? How does the universe respond to what we say? In that same Psalm 139, there is reference to the Most High knowing what I am about to say even before the words reach my lips. My God and I must be one! Why would I have to worry about tomorrow? It happens to us all, but it is not necessary. Look around you. There is so much to love and delight in on Earth. You should never miss the gifts of any day. They are the matters that move emotions and intelligences, that give you reason for wanting to wake again to see and know. Then, of course, you sleep and wake. Is this not marvelous and mysterious at the same time? Your heart teaches you and your body and mind as you sleep, travel, cross vast vistas in heaven and on earth. Well, who cares to make the distinction anymore. I believe the distinction is old. Earth is in heaven. Let's leave this here! Tomorrow. You are right. I did not think, never thought I would lose my sight. I was on my way to becoming, and then the river took a bend. I had to adjust to find later the saying that in faithfulness I was afflicted. Those are comforting from a God of compassion, but the daily grinds of not seeing were rough, to say the least. But after a while, I learned to carry it, even look into it, and subsequently turn it into a major global study touching resourcefulness, compassion and social justice. I never thought this is where I would be before thousands, affecting millions with a story given to me about the eye. It is about flexibility, adaptability because the road is never clear, the path open to cutting by you. There is much to be thankful for now. At least you stand, walk, sit, eat, sleep. But this is not the trouble. You want to become something, someone professional, own your business, your house, have a husband, children, travel, learn, teach, dance, laugh, be safe. What will it be? Will it be a zone of war and disaster or one of peace, love and wisdom? Will it be one of good fruit or one of bitterness, regrets, and hatreds? What does life have to offer? And if your very substance was known and your days even before there was one, I suggest you consult the one who knows it all. And this is surely not me. Even I look into mine for mine. Even I do not know and must ask for understanding to look into laws put in my heart and written on my mind. I must become familiar and move with precision. It is not an easy matter. One Dominican environmentalist told me she had a choice of choosing wisdom or riches and must have heard the Proverbs or the reggae singer named Marley chanting, "Wisdom is better than silver and gold." Following this he intoned, "To the bridge." There was in his cosmology, a need for a bridge between wisdom and silver and gold. It was his reality and indeed, the reality of people of African descent in the Caribbean. Even the Most High knows that riches make a wise person joyful. Is there room for prayer here? Is there room for another matter to be included in prayer? Is one to be chosen over another or is now to be selected over and above all else. This is a long discourse. I long to speak goodness for my people, loved ones, friends, and family and see and know it comes to pass. I've told you before how I hate to see suffering, pain and injustice where people are used by those who came with the intention to use. Those, are they responding to that original purpose? Is this what they came here for? Did the Most High know that that would form part of their purpose? Are they being allowed? And you? You who stand eager to do good, you suffer. This is ancient. Indeed, nothing is new. Within the limited small space for maneuvering, what can you do? Does learning about the belief systems of other cultures help? Does learning a new language change your reality? Another huge discourse. Beloved, I wish I could speak my wish for you and they would come to pass. I want to say I will! When we started this exchange between intelligences I think, never did I think we would be here. Is this not a good thing? It may well disturb, you being twenty-six and I sixty. Many may think whether we thought these exchanges right to do. While we were in them, we did not think so. But we have not read this kind of communication between a man and woman of different ages who have not met and grew to love each other by telephone and email. We decided to take the chance to let others read what happened as we got to know each other. You felt the text as its intensity changed; imagine what those others feel and think! We too were amazed reading it over. How magnificent, we thought boldly. But we had already written it and did not want to waste it. We did not want to delete it either, and when you agreed that it would be great to publish, I was elated. There was so much to think of after deciding to bring this into the public domain, given where we both come from: a small Caribbean society. I can hear the question: Who is Jolita? There will come a time in your life when you should declare that you are the one! It could well be too that Jolita does not exist. She is a product of my imagination. This, I thought, could work. I feel that others would identify her only because I know who she is and she likewise. Does it matter? I toss this out with a flip of my fingers!

I must deal with another exciting matter that never received more than one mention in our exchanges, and that mentioning was made by you. You wrote:

> "I don't think I would be able to do editing. It is too much reading. I am still not halfway your book as yet. Still trying to get there. I love reading, but the time is never there." Then referring to Juliana Jahlee Alfred, you wrote, "She knows her book. I believe if she can imagine what she writes, she can form a picture in her mind that reflects her book or herself. As long as it's something that she feels, she can feel her book through. You know how hard it can be to picture up the right cover. The cover is very important in captivating its readers. It's the first thing you see." Then you wrote that I wrote, 'don't know why I'm writing this to you. I gather you'll have to come up with a creative solution to a particular problem.' "I really do hope that I don't have such problems to solve. I'm not good at solving any

problems unless if its mathematical." I was at the time telling you about Jahlee's book, *Life's Gripes*. She was, at that time, working through creative processes regarding its cover. It was when you said that the only problems you like solving are mathematical ones that I was blown. Wow! I find the 1, 3, 5, 7 kind of pattern formations quite engaging. Mathematics is about patterns, I am reminded. We need a mathematics conversation, beloved! I noticed the nonresponse to such an adventure in your text. You might've hidden it, hoping I spot it. You're a lady who enjoys working with numbers as well as Spanish dance steps, spices, as well as childcare. In your work situation, you deal with percentages, interests, and more. Mathematics and music are close relatives. I am reminded too that numbers have had to exist for us to find them. Where would that place be? Would they be floating in that space of substance, that essential heavenly configuration, one that transcends itself so very often, one that is known and still unknown? I must move on from this once-in-a-lifetime experience, one shared with a woman I may or may not meet in person, in flesh. But I have this strong feeling that I will see and visit you with a basket of fruit: watermelon, pawpaw, cherries, mangos, apricots, and avocados and knock at your door. You ask who is it, and I answer. You open. I enter and lay the box down, stunned!

This is from Jolita:

This started off innocently. Looking back on it all, I am amazed at the thoughts I shared with this man I have never met. I love them all, don't get me wrong. It is just so unreal, from too different times, two completely different people, strangers to each other, yet still through conversation, they became so familiar.

This man has been such an inspiration to me. He drew from me feelings that I never thought I could feel with a complete stranger. The content and depth of our conversations could not have revealed our age at that point in time, our talks on culture, relationships, family, health, and spirituality. It is just an amazing piece to reread.

Frequently, I'd asked you about your eyes and how the healing was coming. I asked because I am curious about what it must be like. I believe that it can be burdensome for someone who has always seen life through their own eyes to not be able to see through these eyes again. Sadly enough, the world doesn't look at people with visual impairment as being the same. You seem to have things figured out: you don't just sit around and wait, you write, you use your computer, you live life as normally as you can. You have developed yourself to a state that it's some - times difficult to even believe that you are impaired. With all these things, you have never lost hope of seeing again. That is truly inspiring.

People have different views as to why and how persons become visually impaired. Like you have heard, it may be a result of sin. That I personally disagree with, 'cause we have all sinned. Where are our punishments to our sins? Is it just some who get punished?

"If we say that we have no sin, we deceive ourselves, and the truth is not in us." (1 John 1:8)

I believe that there is a reason for everything, maybe because of bad choices, or maybe it had to happen so that you could be where you are right now. I know a few kind, thoughtful words can't mend the torn pieces of wanting what we once had. Look at it this way, if things were not as they currently are and you had your perfect sight all through, would you be as reliable as you are today? Would you be just as compassionate? Would you see things the same way you do now? Everything happens in its own season and in its own time. There was a time when you saw through your eyes like me, and now this is the moment when seeing becomes more real, where you see me through my thoughts. When one sense is gone, the other senses are strengthened, and through communicating with you, I have realized that this isn't just a saying, but it is actually true. You sense things in my speech that I would have never revealed to you. It is a blessing. You are blessed with a gift that others do not have, and this is something to hold on to.

You are an inspiration. I do believe this is what drew me to you. Despite all the odds, you fight and never give up, and your fight is one to be recorded. It is inspiring to me and to others. Remember when you came to Dominica to present an address at the Phenomenal Caribbean Men Symposium organized by vfinc?

This story ran in the papers. "I am here as the first movement of my global reach into motivating others to move," you said at the second Phenomenal Caribbean Men Symposium, which was held at the Diocesan Pastoral Center in Morne Bruce, Dominica, on Saturday, November 15, 2014.

A man of his words, what he said, he did, and he lived the example, motivating others to move.

I have been motivated and moved by this man to become the young woman that I am today. My experience with him has taught me that no matter the difficulty, no matter what hinders us from seeing beyond that block, there is a way out. Just hang in there and push through. Let go of what holds you back. Just push through. We are sometimes the biggest setbacks of our life 'cause we allow our self to give up—we tell our self that there is no other recourse. There is *always* a way out.

"Mr. Henry is losing his sight, yes he cried, he fell, he got to the point where it was too much to handle but guess what, he got back up even stronger, not giving up hope but living life and motivating others," the reporter's text intimated.

How can a grown man so distant be so close and have such an impact on a youthful life like mine? Only through our conversations will you be able to answer that.

"There is a beauty in the unseen; it opens up your eyes from deep within." Truly this man was one who had a great passion for beauty. It is normally said that beauty is in the eyes of the beholder, but I must warn you that this beauty I speak of is so much more than the beauty of the eye. He showed me things I never knew existed within me. It is just the way these conversations wrapped and unfolded the true nature of us both: from the surface of our hearts to the depth of our souls!

The passion that we shared was not tamable. I am not talking about a walk-on-the-street acquaintance—his logical way of thinking could have any intelligent person on a quest for truth and belonging.

I thank God every time I think of him, A friend like none other, my instructor, my sails-on lifeboat, my spirit uplifter, my Stein. It is truly a blessing to have this piece available to the public so that people can see that we are all the same. Not age, nor blindness, not even distance can define what true friendship is. We have still never met, and yet he is my closest friend. I am not sure how my boyfriend is going to take this, but Stein is what he is to me, and I thank God for his existence in my life: the love that never grows old.

Love, J.

February 14, 2022

In A Green Night Dawning

Didn't feel it
didn't feel like it
didn't know him anyway
what if he were just another
wanting to
wanting to
truth is I wanted too

imagined too, two bodies soaked in rain now
basking in fire
dripping from a white river
warmed in steam of another water
this one not from him
this one from a lake boiling
in and behind this navel

cut so deep

could not let mama know even see the desire

even as I dreamed it, drank it, sucked it along

interiors in my tongue, heart

and yes, through each thread in breath

itself deeper emptying

deeper

come to see me my love

gaze on moon on my pelvis

many moons

even the one that is thick and dark

telling tales of secrets

in hard trees, hard stones

water-producers

come to see, drink my tenderness my love

I've asked and you have

not responded to the longing

this fecund space set out

like a forest bed for our kissing tongues

on which all creatures love

damp in eco's heat

Is it wrong to think these too

to dress them in pretences or sighs of shyness

chuckles followed by a turn of the tongue

fingers pointing to a gentle need

hidden to this day

this archaeology of desire

we must unearth.

the day comes

your slender, lean form

melted into my warmth

its long historic baths

positioned along corners

touching gentler banks each time

plucking fruity points

each so sweet

yet sweet is not here the word

as breath deepens into central heights upward

as you enter deeper and deeper into that night

of remembrances

full like moons

my thick dark lovely self

so ancient

discovered now

in throes of ecstasy

as we burst into laughter.

there is another thread

to this meeting

no it was not Venus and Mars

was beyond male and female

and beyond

and yes
we both looked
as it flowed out of bodies lifting

I can hear religious screaming
sinner!

it rains, thunders that evening
as tenderness intensified
across thick frontiers of knowing
how joyful
how joyful we were
in the world's most salubrious setting
in a green night dawning!

www.ingramcontent.com/pod-product-compliance
Lightning Source LLC
LaVergne TN
LVHW020412070526
838199LV00054B/3588